MW01036919

AND NOTHING BUT THE TRUTH

And Nothing But the Truth

Jay Sekulow and Keith Fournier

THOMAS NELSON PUBLISHERS
Nashville • Atlanta • London • Vancouver
Printed in the United States of America

Published in Nashville, Tennessee, by Thomas Nelson, Inc., Publishers, and distributed in Canada by Word Communications, Ltd., Richmond, British Columbia.

Sekulow, Jay.

And nothing but the truth : real-life stories of Americans defending their faith and protecting their families / Jay Alan Sekulow and Keith A. Fournier.

p. cm.

"A Janet Thoma Book."

Includes bibliographical references (p.)

ISBN 0-7852-7363-8 (hardcover)

1. Freedom of religion—United States—History—20th century. 2. American Center for Law and Justice. 3. Church and state—United States—History—20th century. 4. United States—Church history—20th century. 5. United States—Politics and government—1993- I. Fournier, Keith A., 1954- . II. Title.

BR516.S44 1996

323.44'2'0973—dc20 96-13156

CIP

Printed in the United States of America.

1 2 3 4 5 6 — 01 00 99 98 97 96

To my mother, Natalie Sekulow, the person who can out talk me.
Jay Alan Sekulow

This book is lovingly dedicated to my wife, Laurine. Her faithful companionship through all these years is the bedrock of my life. She is my best friend, my bride, and my partner in faith and ministry. She is also a wonderful mother and co-pastor to our domestic church, Kristen, Keith Jr., Ann, Mary Ellen, and Joel, our wonderful children.
Keith A. Fournier

Acknowledgments

Special appreciation is extended to the Reverend Robert L. Wise, Ph.D., for his work as part of our team. Dr. Wise spent countless hours researching our files, previous cases, and notes developing a comprehensive picture of our work. His interviews of clients provided much of the material in these chapters. He helped us focus on our story. His editorial assistance and writing gifts shaped this literary picture of our work.

The Reverend Paul Chaim Schenck, L.H.D.; Joel Thornton; A. J. Cortman; and Debra Kiggins have faithfully assisted in the task of helping Dr. Wise with the development of the manuscript. In addition, we have been blessed with the services of Janet Thoma, one of the finest editors in the publishing business.

Jay Alan Sekulow and Keith A. Fournier

Contents

PART 1

A TIME FOR NEW BEGINNINGS

CHAPTER 1

TAKING THE HIGH GROUND

AIMEE IS the sort of second grader you have to love. Sweet, gentle, and innocent, she started mastering the world of computers at about the time kids once started learning arithmetic. Unfortunately, the personnel at Krene De Los Lagos School, Tempe, Arizona, thought Aimee had a behavior problem.

The difficulty started on a Thursday morning in March 1995. Aimee was sitting in the computer lab working on exercises to familiarize her with the keyboard. The bright, inquisitive child took the initiative and started typing in words. By the time the teacher came by and looked over her shoulder, Aimee had typed on the screen "Jesus." Aimee loved this name and used it daily in prayer. Like writing the name of her best friend, she had typed in the most natural expression she knew.

Mrs. Perry froze in her tracks and immediately admonished Aimee for typing in *such* an unacceptable word! Aimee was instructed to fill out a behavior report for the misdeed. The child was shocked but, as always, obedient. Under the heading "This Is What I Did," Aimee wrote, "I rote Jesus on the computer. Jesus not exsceptical on computers." The final section of the discipline slip required Aimee to identify a rule to be remembered. She circled the "need to cooperate with teachers." For her gross misbehavior, Aimee was given a yellow warning light indicating marginal behavior for the entire day.

Unable to comprehend what she had done wrong, Aimee did not tell her parents about the disciplinary action for several days. Is it right for second graders to live in fear of using the language and words they learn in Sunday school?

Meet Joseph DiBiase and his friends in the Teens for Christ Bible Club in, of all places, Nazareth (Pennsylvania) High School. The committed thirteen-year-old formed what would seem to be the best kind of activity for teenagers. In a time when gangs, drugs, violence, and smuggled guns are the principal concerns of school administrators, one would expect a school to applaud a Bible club. Not so!

In January, the usual announcements were made over the high school intercom calling for groups to have their pictures taken for the annual yearbook. Joseph listened as the Key Club, Students Against Drunk Driving, the Animal and Earth Club, and the Drama Club were scheduled. He waited quietly. Surely the administrator didn't mean to overlook the Teens for Christ Bible Club. But no other announcements for pictures were called.

Joseph immediately went to the office to talk with the principal. To his amazement, he heard the following explanation. "Sorry, Joseph, due to the religious nature of Teens for Christ, they just can't be included in the yearbook." Joseph couldn't believe his ears. He and his friends were left out in the cold for being "religious."

What in the world is going on? We must take a second long look at the religious struggle going on in America today.

The past century has been one of unparalleled conflict. Contemporary Americans cannot escape the legacy of battle and strife. When World War I was fought "over there," the sounds of battle were inaudible and relatively impersonal. By 1940, World War II was far more immediate, and virtually every American family was touched by the conflict. Still, the average citizen was separated from actual conflict by an ocean. Geographic isolation left American homes unscathed.

Matters changed with the cold war. Intercontinental missiles made the heartland of the United States vulnerable. Nothing and no one was exempt from the ever-present threat of nuclear war. We learned to be terrified of the possibility of military conflict and personal loss.

With the fall of the Berlin Wall and the demise of the Marxist state, Americans sighed and settled back into affluence and personal satisfaction. Many forgot that they had survived an undeclared World War III. Christians thanked God for providential protection and went back to the business of being Ozzie and Harriet, David and Ricky. Few realized a silent but equally significant struggle was already underway: a struggle for the nation's soul!

Make no mistake: The new battleground is on your front porch and in your living room. The battle comes in every day with the newspaper, through your television set. Skirmishes are fought daily in the schools, in front of abortion clinics, in public gathering places, in Congress, in courtrooms, and on television. The weapons are ideology and propaganda. Although words take the place of bullets, the strife can be just as fierce.

But the battle isn't new or peculiar to the last half of this century. For two thousand years Christians have been locked into the same struggle for the conversion of their society. Today we are fighting the adversary in a relatively new form. Called secularism, the issue is the place of Judeo-Christian values in government, in the schools, in the media, and throughout national life. The conflict isn't over whether we will have public values but over whose values will prevail.

The forces of secularism, modernism, and a politically correct elitism are relentlessly at work to establish a viewpoint in the American mind. Some of the forces come in the form of politicians while others are dressed as lawyers. Frequently they are camouflaged as clerics and speak from the pulpits of churches. Often the opposition teaches kindergarten or a political science class in a small rural high school. The opposition is represented in the universities and on the school boards all over the land. The objective of this new struggle is a cultural consensus that would displace Judeo-Christian values and stifle religious expression in the public sector.

This contemporary struggle is as significant and the consequences as far reaching in determining who we shall be as a nation as any military campaign fought in our history as a nation.

A Culture of Death

Face the facts. A price is being paid this very minute. The result of the shift in values in our schools and homes is now spelled out on the streets in blood. Teenage gangs terrorize entire neighborhoods and kill each other daily. Prime-time television offers nightly advanced courses in violence. The death we see on the nightly news, however, is nothing compared to the slaughter of the unborn being hidden behind the doors of abortion clinics. Because they don't hear bombs dropping or smell death in the air, most people assume the battle of words is inconsequential. Nothing could be further from the truth!

Rhetoric of conflict and disagreement is always the deadly preface to actual physical engagement. Wars begin in parliaments long before they are fought on farm meadows. The first blows are always struck with ideas and are only later translated into clashing swords and flying missiles.

Our present struggle is no different. That's one reason Pat Robertson founded the American Center for Law and Justice (the ACLJ, a public interest law firm committed to pro-liberty, pro-life, and pro-family causes). Jay Alan Sekulow is the chief counsel of the ACLJ. As primary litigator, in a few years he has been before the Supreme Court more times than most attorneys could dream of in a lifetime. Through his television and radio programs he is heard across America each week by millions of Americans. Keith A. Fournier is the founding executive director of the center. In addition to leading the center, he is the philosopher and "apologist" for the ACLJ, articulating its mission and position and charting its course as its visionary. Keith has been a prime mover in bringing together the members of both Roman Catholic, Protestant, and Orthodox Christian communities in their mutual struggle to preserve religious freedom. He is often co-counsel in issues before the Supreme Court.

If you think ideological assertions and political decisions are unimportant, consider again the cost of this current American conflict.

Aimee Karger had to struggle with feelings of doubt for days. If her situation had not been challenged, a badly misinformed teacher would have gone on her way treating the name of Jesus as profanity. A climate of religious persecution would have persisted.

Fortunately, Nancy Karger, Aimee's mother, wrote a letter to the school superintendent expressing her serious concern over the teacher's actions. "I find it interesting that talking in class didn't warrant a yellow warning, yet her displaying a personal religious being—a person's right—was met with such a negative reaction."

Once our team at the American Center for Law and Justice was contacted, we investigated and found Aimee was punished for only one reason. She had used a "religious" word. The teacher's action was blatant discrimination. We reminded the school that in the 1967 *Shelton v. Tucker* case, the Supreme Court of the United States held that "the vigilant protection of constitutional freedom is nowhere more vital than in the community of American schools." We called the school system's attention to the fact that a student's free speech rights apply whether "a student is in the cafeteria, or in the playing field or on campus during authorized hours."

We closed our letter to the school by demanding justice for Aimee. Nothing less than destroying all disciplinary records of this incident was acceptable. We asked for a written apology from the teacher.

The school district first tried to change the facts but finally apologized. Mrs. Perry also expressed regrets. We put the school on notice that our West Coast office would continue to monitor the situation. The ACLJ would not allow them to avoid taking full responsibility for their actions.

Aimee's case is not an isolated incident. In 1993, Adam Villa simply wanted to sing the Christian song "Shepherd Boy" in a school talent show. School officials refused his request until our legal team intervened. Two years earlier Luanne Fulbright was told her report on baby Jesus violated the separation of church and state and couldn't be displayed. If Christians had not stood their ground, a wedge would have been driven between them and their rights. Presence and witness would have been lost.

We cannot forget Edmund Burke's warning. "All that is needed for evil to succeed, is for good men to do nothing."

The time is long overdue for Christians to confront our culture of death and transform it from within into a culture of life and hope. Not just for ourselves, but for all who cherish freedom, life, and the family.

The Teens for Christ Bible Club recognized a battlefield in the center of their school building. Prayerfully, Joseph and his friends skated out on thin ice and decided to confront the powers that be. Heady stuff for teenagers! They called us and asked the ACLJ to advise them about their rights and how to proceed.

We drafted a letter and sent it to the attorneys for the Nazareth, Pennsylvania, school board. As the ACLJ had done many times in the past, we explained the Equal Access Act, which guarantees religious groups the same opportunity in taxpayer funded buildings as all others. Christian students can't be treated like second-class citizens or marginalized in the public sector. Religious faith doesn't prevent Christian groups from gaining access to normal means of public expression.

School district lawyers took a long second look at our position and set out a new policy for the public school system. They wrote: "Personnel at the high school indicated that they would be able to have the photographer return and that inclusion would not be a major problem." The Teens for Christ had their picture taken and appeared in the yearbook.

After the matter was settled, Joe DiBiase sent a thank you letter to our senior trial counsel, Stuart Roth. Joe wrote: "When God was leading me toward the possibility of putting together a Bible club, I saw Jay talking about them, and I'll never forget what he said. He said something like this: 'I have won the right for the students, but it is up to them to act upon it.' Freedom is gained in vain if no one takes advantage of it."

As Christians we must be people of action. Too much ground has been lost by allowing secular, anti-religious forces to abridge or deny religious freedom to people of faith and all American citizens of goodwill. It is time to recover what has been lost and to establish religious freedom, the sanctity of life, and the primacy of the family in American society.

Today a defense and counterattack movement has begun to take shape across America. The ACLU can no longer assume the rights of Christians and other people of faith to be an easy target. Politically correct politicians can't discriminate against religious people without being challenged. We are meeting our opponents on their own turf and winning.

Now it's time for you to recognize your place in the struggle and identify how you can make a difference in your local community. In the following chapters we will equip you to make a difference at this crucial moment.

CHAPTER 2

NEW BEGINNINGS

WE TRACE the struggle back to March 3, 1987. That afternoon Jay had just finished successfully defending the Jews for Jesus airport evangelism case before the Supreme Court of the United States. Secularism was determined to silence the witness for the gospel in the marketplace. Jay demonstrated freedom of speech covered the religious arena as well as the political. The journey of a thousand miles began with this first step.

When the issue of passing out Jews for Jesus literature in the Los Angeles International Airport first arose, Jay didn't feel the matter was substantial. For fourteen years, the organization had been working there when suddenly the airport police threatened to arrest one of the missionaries. Again, Jay felt the issue wouldn't go far, as every court in the land had ruled airports were acceptable places for such contacts. Everyone from the Moonies to the Hare Krishnas had been allowed through the door. So, what was the big deal?

Much more was at work than met the eye. The opposition was determined to shut down the Christian witnesses. Many people felt that God wanted Jay on the case. At the same time, Jay's practice took a nosedive. Sudden changes in regulations caused the collapse of his real estate business. He was surrounded by a mass of contradictions.

Only in retrospect could Jay discern that God was truly at work creating a new beginning. At the point where he could control nothing, Jay had no choice but to acquiesce completely to the will of God. He plunged into preparations to take the airport case all the way to the Supreme Court.

Jay's curiosity about why the case went to the Supreme Court would not be denied. "Nothing personal," he said to the opposing lawyer, "but why is the city of Los Angeles pushing this case all the way to the top?" Jay assumed the 1984 Olympics created concerns.

The L.A. city attorney shrugged. The airport commissioners wanted to test the regulations. Maybe we could change something. Jay is convinced that Jews for Jesus was picked because the airport commissioners didn't think Christians would put up much of a fight.

Jay was before the Supreme Court for only thirty minutes in his first case. The justices sliced the L.A. city attorney to pieces. When it was over, a new direction was established. The court unanimously upheld the decision of the lower court that the airport's actions were unconstitutional. Christians *had* fought back and won. Tides were turning.

On March 3, 1987, standing on the steps of the United States Supreme Court, Jay listened as Moishe Rosen, executive director of Jews for Jesus, gave a prophetic word. "You will be back here often." Jay chuckled. Most lawyers never appear before the Supreme Court in a lifetime. Little did Jay know the entrance would become a revolving door.

Why was Jay Sekulow appearing on behalf of Jews for Jesus before the Supreme Court of the land? The irony of God was at work on that spring afternoon. In 1956, Jay was born in Brooklyn, New York, into a Jewish family. Growing up in the synagogue, Jay knew how to keep Sabbath and attended Hebrew School. From his reading of the Old and New Testaments, Jay found Jesus as his personal Messiah. As eighteen-year-old Jay listened to the Liberated Wailing Wall, a Jews for Jesus singing group, he was moved to personal commitment. This decision shaped his faith, life, and vocation.

The airport evangelism case was only the prelude to fighting for the right of prayer and Bible clubs to meet in the nation's public schools. In the beginning, the concern was only a small trickle of interest. Today reports indicate there are more than twelve thousand Bible and intercessor groups meeting on school campuses. We still remain committed to fighting for *any* student group denied access to their school's property.

The airport evangelism case was followed by an assault on

beach evangelism. Teaming up with senior counsel Pat Monaghan's Free Speech Advocates, Jay went to court in Texas and won. Waiting next in line was a group of twenty-four Christians under attack for praying on a public sidewalk in front of an abortion clinic in Atlanta. When we prevailed in Georgia, we knew we were on to an approach of considerable significance.

In 1990, Beverly LaHaye asked Jay to oversee the legal department of Concerned Women for America. Paul and Jan Crouch called on the Trinity Broadcasting Network (TBN) family to surround our work with prayer. American Christians had begun the fight to preserve their constitutional freedoms.

A New Vision Is Born

Keith Fournier and his family left on a well deserved holiday at Lake of the Woods, Virginia. After years as general counsel, as well as dean of students, dean of evangelization, and presidential assistant, at Franciscan University of Steubenville, he was feeling the need for something different. The rest of the family was at the right place for a change as well. Keith's friend Chuck Colson had recommended some possible new options, but the fundamental issue was always the same. How could he continue to integrate evangelism, cultural apologetics, and the practice of law? Heavy questions for a time apart with the family.

A short side trip up to Virginia Beach sounded like a good diversion. Keith wanted to see how Pat Robertson's effort to work Christian principles into professional legal education was developing at Regent University.

When Keith pulled into the stately campus of Regent University and the Christian Broadcasting Network (CBN) complex, he was deeply impressed with the grandeur of the Georgian architecture. The place had the feel of permanency, significance. Excitement was in the air. For the first time, Keith heard from the law school's dean the plans to gather Christian lawyers who could confront the ACLU and similar groups wreaking havoc on the nation.

"I'm all too familiar with these misguided public-interest cliques trying to change the cultural landscape during the last thirty years," Keith responded. "They have besieged the courts with strategic test cases to use the First Amendment to censor the free speech of people of faith." He added, "Whatever they perceive as religious or particularly Christian is deemed politically incorrect."

"Exactly!" The dean shook his finger vigorously. "In contrast, we are developing the concept of a legal center for a counteroffensive to stop the erosion of our rights. You need to talk to several other people working here at Regent."

In the next few hours, Keith talked with the chancellor of the university, the president of CBN, the chairman of the board of the Family Channel, and the founder of the Christian Coalition and the ACLJ. By the end of the day, Keith had chatted with Pat Robertson for almost two hours.

The broad outline of a public-interest law firm was sketched before Keith. The American Center for Law and Justice would be a gathering place for lawyers who believed that the constitutional right to true religious and civil liberty involved governmental accommodations of religious faith and practice, not hostility. The center would fight for the rightful place of religious faith in American society as well as the primacy of the family and the sanctity and dignity of all human life.

Keith found in Pat Robertson an astute, intelligent, passionate, and concerned citizen and leader. He was a bold entrepreneur and founder. Keith was deeply challenged and moved by what he saw, heard, and believed was possible.

At the close of the meeting, Pat asked, "Keith, what would it take to get you here?"

"What . . . what . . . do you mean?" Keith stammered. He was immediately aware that his Roman Catholic Christian faith could be a possible obstacle in this evangelical Protestant setting.

"Would you consider becoming the executive director of the American Center for Law and Justice?"

"Pat, this is a surprise. I am honored but . . . " Keith began thinking of his five kids facing college, his awareness that the center would have to start on a shoestring budget. "I will have to give this idea a lot of thought."

"And prayer," Pat added.

"Of course."

Suddenly they were praying on the spot.

Laurine and Keith spent the rest of the vacation in deep conversations, long prayers, and reflection. By the next Monday, Keith was back in court as juvenile prosecutor for Jefferson County, Ohio. Teenagers caught dealing in crack cocaine were on the docket. Bureau of Criminal Investigation representatives were ready to testify, and phones were ringing everywhere. One of the calls was from Pat Robertson. At 6:00 P.M., Keith and Pat finally connected.

"Hello, Keith," Pat began. "I'd like to invite you to become the executive director of the American Center for Law and Justice. It's going to be big."

Keith and Laurine had already come to the point of decision. They had been through the meat grinder of Christian ministries and career changes, riding the waves of excitement and failure. No longer were they starry-eyed dreamers discounting risk without giving any thought to the cost.

After prayer and seeking the counsel of close friends and trusted peers, they closed the law practice, sold their home, and moved to Virginia Beach. New beginnings were underway.

A short time later, in June of 1991, Keith and Jay met at a Christian lawyers' meeting in Washington, D.C., and talks followed. We immediately recognized a kindred mindset. In our second meeting, we established a basis for cooperating on cases. Common cause was forming. Two streams of concern with diverse approaches were flowing together. A partnership was emerging.

Freedom Fighters

The ACLJ started taking shape around two old wooden desks and some used furniture from a Virginia Beach secondhand furniture store. Crammed in two back offices in a Regent classroom with two part-time graduate student staffers, Keith recognized the time had come to reclaim the term "public-interest law." Many such groups operated in anything *but* the best interests of the public. The ACLJ would be pro-liberty, pro-life, and pro-family. Public interest law would again be practiced for the good of the whole society.

We began working together on a case-by-case basis. Earlier Jay had formed a religious-liberty organization called Christian Advocates Serving Evangelism (CASE). CASE became the Atlanta office of the ACLJ. As Jay became chief counsel for the entire ACLJ effort, new beach heads were forged.

Confrontation in Canada

The lessons of Jay's first Supreme Court battle extended beyond America's borders. The necessity to resist was tested in 1992 north of the border. Fortunately, concerned Canadian Christians were already at work to provide a common platform for facing their struggle for religious freedom.

The Canadian Center for Law and Justice (CCLJ) opened in Ottawa with a service of worship and praise. The frigid January temperatures didn't dampen the spirit of the gathering inside St. James Anglican Church. Anglicans, Methodists, Presbyterians, Pentecostals, Roman Catholics, Eastern Orthodox, and members of evangelical confessions prayed with one voice in gratitude and hope for the new effort. Keith and senior counsel Thomas P. Monaghan represented the ACLJ. Gerard and Renald Guay accepted the reins of leadership for the CCLJ.

The group knew well that the Canadian Charter of Rights and Freedoms promulgated in 1982 guaranteed freedom of conscience and religion. Freedom of the press as well as other media of communication and freedom of thought, belief, opinion, and expression were ensured. In both English and French, Gerard proclaimed the Canadian Center's intent to take the document seriously and to stand against the rising tide of intolerant secularism.

The first big challenge was not long in coming. The Canadian federal government seized transmitting equipment from several twenty-four-hour Christian television stations, including a church in Medicine Hat, Alberta, alleging these broadcasters were operating illegally. As a matter of fact, they were operating without licenses because it is impossible for any solely Christian broadcaster to obtain a television broadcasting permit in Canada.

Pastor Roy Beyer's church was one of the places raided by the government. Victory Christian Fellowship had developed a unique leadership style in the Alberta region. Pastor Beyer knew the potential of Christian witness over the airways. He said, "No form of media has a greater effect in terms of what people believe and how they think than . . . television."

And yet the pastor was caught in a strange quagmire. The Canadian Radio/Television and Telecommunications Commission (CRT) allowed all-rock music stations, all-sports stations, all-movie stations, but there was no room for an all-Christian station. Some of the stations taken off the air were broadcasting programs from Trinity Broadcasting Network—a very strange contradiction of the Canadian Charter of Rights and Freedoms.

With the resources of the ACLJ behind them, Gerard Guay and his staff went to work developing a strategy to change the existing laws. The Canadian Center participated in CRT hearings and pressed their point. They made progress, but the new religious broadcasting policy still discriminated against religious groups. The final showdown came when the CCLJ filed a lawsuit against the CRT for its religious broadcasting policy. In their pleadings, the CCLJ noted these policies violate the Canadian Charter of Rights and Freedoms. On October 14, 1994, the CRT reversed field and changed their long-held position. Religious broadcasting licenses were issued to two radio stations in Montreal and Québec City.

Gerard Guay responded, "We rejoice that for the first time in close to seventy years, Christian stations will be authorized to operate in Canada."

In just two short years, the CCLJ had come from seeing Christian stations seized to the licensing of religious radio stations. However, the license applicants still must conform to the religious broadcasting policy code of the state. The CRT position continues to be an unconstitutional restriction of the freedom of expression, religion, and association. Still a barrier has been knocked down, and broadcasting is going forth across a nation where 80 percent of the population defines itself as Christian. A new day has begun, and training for a new generation of lawyers.

A Cadre of Young Lawyers

Don Lawrence and Dave Cortman are examples of the new breed of lawyers studying at Regent University. They are helping the ACLJ create chapters of Christian students in law schools and have their own message for other students across the country. Each man is a leader in developing a new legal environment.

David Cortman, a former Youth for Christ leader, is a bright guy with dark, piercing eyes. "The Law Student Advocates Association is a new movement we are establishing in law schools across the land," he says. "Every chapter is a place for Christians to come together and join in common cause. We are organizing units all over this country to make sure that students have the opportunity to hear the Christian perspective *while* they are in training."

Keith explains, "We are raising up a new generation of advocates. Our goal at the ACLJ is to have a long-range impact on what is happening in America. These young men and women will carry the torch of religious freedom forward into the third millennium of Christianity."

Don Lawrence, a tall, earnest young man, came to Regent to be part of changing America. Don explains, "I am a law student today because I saw a pressing need for Christian lawyers. My goal is not only to impact culture but to transform it. I'm making my Christian witness through my profession."

Reaching for Tomorrow

Today the ACLJ has, in addition to its full-time lawyers in five offices, five hundred affiliates throughout the nation—Catholic, Protestant, Orthodox, and Messianic Jewish in their confessional identification. The Canadian work continues through the CCLJ. The Law Student Advocates Program now has chapters at some of the most prestigious law campuses in America, including Notre Dame, Harvard, Emory, Detroit Mercy, and Duquesne, as well as Regent University. Our goal is to have a chapter on every law school campus in the country.

How do new beginnings happen? Sometimes with as simple a matter as a vision. One of Keith's favorite passages comes from the prophet Habakkuk. He wrote, "For the vision is yet for an appointed time; but at the end it will speak, and it will not lie. Though it tarries, wait for it; because it will surely come, it will not tarry."[1]

What finally turns the tides? The hand of God.

CHAPTER 3

AMERICA'S CULTURE OF DISBELIEF

AN ALASKAN school district issued new instructions to the students recently. They were forbidden to say "Merry Christmas." Instead, they were instructed to give "Season's Greetings."

Cindy Pedington discovered that the same crusade to take Christ out of Christmas had come to her hometown. The annual light parade through Christmas Island near Somerset, Kentucky, attracted hundreds of tourists. But Cindy noticed something was missing. Among the thousands of displays in every conceivable shape there was not one nativity scene. When Cindy asked about the oversight she was told that public policy banned any religious statements. The ACLU would sue to prohibit anything that looked like a nativity scene. Only by calling on the American Center for Law and Justice was Cindy able to stop the attempts to neutralize Christmas on Christmas Island.

In northern California another strange story emerged. As the Advent season approached, a grade school choir began preparing Christmas music for a school performance. The traditional carol "Joy to the World" was selected, and practice began.

Morgan Smith recognized something strange as she began rehearsing. Key words had been marked out. Every time a religious word like *savior, king,* or *Lord* appeared, it was blacked out. The music teacher instructed the students just to hum at those places. Morgan was mystified: The deletions made the verses sound silly, like a game in which the listener was to guess what the original words were.

"What's the point of the humming?" Morgan asked.

"We can't do the religious stuff," the teacher answered. "Sing it like I've marked the page. Let's begin." The music director started the practice again.

Other students quickly realized how incongruous the piece was without the traditional words. Many began singing the words anyway. The irritated teacher stopped the group.

"Any one of you who sings 'Jesus,' 'Lord,' or 'savior' will be kicked out of the choir," she asserted. "Sing the piece the altered way or leave."

Stunned, Morgan took the piece home to her mother. Mrs. Smith was outraged. Her family's Christian heritage was being denied by what they were asking her daughter to do. When Mrs. Smith confronted the principal, he explained that the changes were his idea. "The words might offend someone," he said. When Mrs. Smith told him *she* was offended by these actions, the principal defended his position. "I advise the teachers to avoid anything that is *too* religious," he concluded.

What's the Problem?

With the Berlin Wall down, Communism discredited, and "In God We Trust" printed on American money, why should anyone have to be concerned over religious expression in this country?

Because we have lived through a gigantic cultural shift not unlike the slippage in the San Andreas fault in California. Life in America isn't what the framers of the Constitution intended. The tremors seen on TV and felt in the home and in the public schools are the consequences of the emergence of a new culture of disbelief.

Family historians Becky Glass and Margaret Stolee discovered that many of the proposed reforms in family law have frightening precedent in another attempt at revolutionary change at the beginning of this century. When the Bolsheviks came to power in the Soviet Union, they initiated easy divorce, abolished the distinction between legitimate and illegitimate births, collectivized child care, and redefined the family. Marxists believed dismantling the family was a necessary step in creating a classless society. Social theorists were attempting to build a culture of disbelief.[1]

And what happens when such attempts succeed? Psychiatrist Boris Segal discovered that as the family deteriorates a crisis in society follows. With the decline of the authority of the Church and disillusionment with religious ideas comes a loss of a sense of continuity and belonging. Increasing alienation, antagonism, delinquency, personal destructiveness, drug use, teenage pregnancies, runaways, school dropouts, teen suicide, and violent crime naturally result. Sociologist Viktor Grecas discovered that the outcome of family disorder is a growing appetite for themes of "violence, nihilism, and exploitative sex."[2]

When Christians can no longer influence their culture with values derived from their faith, the culture that emerges is hopeless, utilitarian, materialistic, and hollow. Today we are witnessing the results at the highest levels of national life. In a syndicated newspaper column, Keith responded to statements made by President Bill Clinton about his own personal beliefs.

The president humbly declared himself to be a Christian, "an honest struggling believer, trying to grow everyday, trying to learn more everyday, never pretending to be anything other than I am." Keith took Mr. Clinton at his word but noted that granting sincerity to the president's statements raised other critical issues. How does the faith of the president shape and influence his politics, his public policies? Does his stated personal commitment to Jesus Christ make any difference in his public actions?

When we understand the Christian view of the dignity and

rights of every human being, born or unborn, it becomes clear that these bedrock convictions must be translated into very different positions than those of President Clinton's administration.

We are faced with many anti-liberty ideas packaged as enlightened hedonism promoting pleasure and singular self-fulfillment. Many of these actions result in escalating crime and the demise of moral conscience, literally tearing asunder our social fabric. Such is the shadow side of a culture of disbelief.

The Founders' Intent

The University of Houston investigated more than fifteen thousand writings of the founding fathers from 1760 to 1805 to determine the origins of their ideas. Three men quoted most often were Montesquieu, John Locke, and William Blackstone. Yet the Bible was quoted *sixteen times* more frequently than Locke and Blackstone. In 94 percent of the documents, scripture was quoted.

The ACLU and similar groups have launched disinformation campaigns regarding how the doctrine of separation of church and state should be interpreted. Because many people do not correctly grasp the essence of the idea of separation, misinterpretation has quickly led to chaos. Hunting season is open.

Try this civic quiz and see how you score. Which of the following passages is from the U.S. Constitution?

"Congress shall make no law respecting an establishment of religion, or prohibiting the free exercise thereof."

"In order to ensure to citizens freedom of conscience, the church is separated from the state, and the school from the church. Freedom of religious worship is recognized for all citizens."

A majority of Americans are able to identify the first statement as coming from the Constitution. But many are shocked to discover the second statement is from the Soviet constitution.

Surprised? Consider another fact. A poll of the American public revealed two-thirds of the citizens believe that the phrase "separation of church and state" is in the Constitution. It isn't.

In the First Amendment to the Bill of Rights, Congress was forbidden to make law "respecting an establishment of religion, or prohibiting the free exercise thereof." In fact, the phrase "separation of church and state" did not appear until 1802 when Thomas Jefferson corresponded to a Baptist congregation in Danbury, Connecticut. It appears that the so-called civil libertarians have quietly amended their copies of the First Amendment to add Jefferson's now well-known little phrase.

The Infamous Wall

Religious cleansers have magnified Jefferson's expression into an unscalable "wall of separation doctrine" justifying every attack on the guaranteed free exercise of religion. As secularists propagated their skewed interpretations of separation, they began creating the new climate.

While religious cleansers would disavow this interpretation, what has actually happened has been an attack of one religion on another. Christianity has been under siege by the new religion called secularism. Rather than introduce "religionlessness," the opposition is bent on instilling secular humanism as the prevailing national religion. They have absolutely no intent whatsoever of separating *this* religion from the state. That's why as Christians we so often become the targets of their efforts to restructure the culture.

The new barriers created by the secularists have imprisoned religious speech. For example, on the corner of Forty-third and Broadway in New York City two pastors were arrested for preaching the gospel during the 1992 Christmas season. They were charged with disorderly conduct, until the ACLJ got the charges dropped. Ironically, they would have had more freedom on the streets of Moscow!

Shortly after the Berlin Wall fell, a colleague gave Keith a piece of the wall. The effect on Keith of receiving this symbol of recovered freedom was profound. He immediately recalled Ronald Reagan standing at the wall on June 12, 1987, and boldly addressing Mikhail Gorbachev on behalf of the entire free world. "Mr. Gorbachev, tear down this wall!" On that New Year's Eve, as the ball dropped in Times Square, the hammer and sickle fell in Moscow.

Now the time has come for the wall to fall in this land. We cannot allow religion to be taken from our public life. This religious censorship must come to an end. The ACLJ has never wanted, worked for, or given any encouragement to the idea of the government endorsing one—or any—form of religion. But by the same token we don't want hostility toward faith and religious speech.

In 1952, Justice William Douglas warned in *Zorach v. Clauson* about hostility. "We cannot read into the Bill of Rights such a philosophy of hostility of religion." In 1984, Chief Justice Warren Burger added this concern: "Such hostility would bring us into war with our national tradition as embodied in the First Amendment's guaranty of the free exercise of religion."[3] That war has begun.

Millions of Americans are remembering the words of President Reagan: "Tear down this wall!" and are applying them now to this context of religious hostility. They cry out, "Let our children pray and our preachers preach. Allow our citizens to express their heritage at Christmas time." Even though our society is increasingly pluralistic, we must ensure an equal playing field rather than a religiously cleansed arena where people of faith are no longer welcome.

Turning Things Around

Sometimes we must take matters into our own hands to stop the continuing slide into darkness.

The New York City South Street Seaport area has always been a popular tourist haunt. As is true of the Atlantic coastal area from New York City north, the streets and docks reflect the earliest history of the country. Cobblestones and colorful port scenery remind people of where and how the country began.

The millions coming to South Street Seaport often found a unique expression of freedom going on in the streets. Concerned evangelical Christians shared their faith by handing out tracts and witnessing verbally. But in 1988, security guards muscled in with a new version of the law. No more witnessing on the streets and sidewalks! Religious freedom no longer applied on South Street.

Where did the police come from?

During the development of the area, the Rouse Corporation had actually leased the sidewalk from the city. Rouse had come to consider the public area their personal preserve. Company security people functioned like private police. Even when Jay responded as an attorney for witnessing Christians, the harassment didn't stop.

Jay finally indulged in a little civil disobedience to confront the issues fully. He joined the group, passed out tracts, and became one of the New York evangelists. Sure enough! Jay was quickly numbered among the offenders.

Jay threatened to obtain a temporary restraining order against the company to guarantee the group's right to continue witnessing. He furiously researched the issues, looking for just the right angle. He sifted through hundreds of pages of legal documents, briefs, and previous opinions until he found a key insight. Regardless of who controls the sidewalk, First Amendment activities could not be denied! The Rouse Corporation could not legally suppress free speech.

As soon as Jay pressed the constitutional ramifications of the repression, the South Street lawyers were forced to concede. A handful of evangelical Christians had taken on a company over what is unquestionably a fundamental right and won a major victory. Like the civil disobedience that played a key role in forming this nation, the courage of a few has opened a door for the many.

Recovering Perspective

What does one say to this current culture of disbelief? President Woodrow Wilson had a poignant reminder for us: "A nation which does not remember what is was yesterday, does not know what it is today, nor what it is trying to do. We are trying to do a futile thing if we do not know where we came from or what we have been about."[4]

Where did we come from and what were we about? Look again at our national beginnings.

On Virginia's sandy beaches where the Chesapeake Bay joins the Atlantic Ocean is the site where the unfolding drama of the United States began. On April 29, 1607, British colonists landed at what they called Cape Henry. The first act of these 120 initial immigrants was to plant a wooden cross in the ground, kneel, and ask for God's blessing on this land. They arose to pursue their mission to bring morality to these shores through education and religion. In their charter of colonization they stated their intent clearly. They wanted to propagate "Christian Religion to such people, as is yet in Darkness and miserable ignorance of the true knowledge and worship of God, and may in time bring the infidels and savage, living in those parts, to human civility, and to a settled and quiet government."[5] Clearly, the United States of America began as a culture of conviction, not neutrality.

The cross-planting incident was not singular. Less than a hundred miles away on March 25, 1634, two more ships came from England bringing more refugees from religious persecution. They landed on St. Clement's Island in the Potomac River. Father White, leader of the expedition, recorded their first actions in his diary: "We celebrated Mass. . . . This had never been done before in this part of the world. After we had completed, we took on our shoulders a great cross, which we had hewn out of a tree, and advancing in order to the appointed place, with the assistance of the Governor and his associates . . . we erected a trophy to Christ the savior."[6]

As had been true earlier in Virginia, the new Maryland settlement, at the very least, saw no problem in church and state existing side by side in harmony and partnership. Moreover, the founders saw the need for both church and state to work together to build a better world than the one they had left behind in Europe.

The colonists landed on Plymouth Rock in Massachusetts espousing the same intentions. Sailing from Holland in search of religious liberty, the pilgrims forged their way through the wilderness with profound intent. In 1647, leader William Bradford wrote in his *Of Plymouth Plantation:* "Last and not least, they cherished a great hope and inward zeal of laying good foundations, or at least some ways toward it, for the propagation and advance of the gospel of the kingdom of Christ in the remote parts of the world, even though they should be but stepping stones to others in the performances of so great a work."[7] When the founders of Massachusetts and Connecticut made the first school laws in 1642 and 1647, their expressed intention was to teach children to read and write in order to understand the scriptures. The Bible was their textbook.[8]

Harvard was founded in 1636 with the stated purpose and intent that students would come to know God and Jesus as the way to eternal life. The same was true of Yale, Princeton, and the original universities that comprised the American higher education system. Scripture reading was mandatory.

The foregoing is what our nation was yesterday. The nation arose from men and women gathered around crosses in prayer. Light years away from a culture of disbelief, the American experiment began in prayer meetings and Communion services.

Presenting and Maintaining the Higher Way

It is not an accident of history that evangelical Pat Robertson, Roman Catholic Keith Fournier, and Messianic Jew Jay Sekulow stand together at this moment of history to proclaim and defend the Christian faith.

Their answer is a three-pronged response restoring liberty, life, and family. Remembering Nehemiah's call not to be afraid as the wall of Jerusalem was rebuilt, the ACLJ is following a similar strategy of erecting again the wall of civility in a decaying, secularized culture. The task began in exposing the moral foundations of this nation. Like the ancient workmen fighting with a spear in one hand and a trowel in the other, we build and spar with the opposition at the same time. Rebuilding and contending are the dual task of the hour.

Using the sword of litigation, the ACLJ fends off social marauders trying to strip away the remnants of our civilization. Groups attack under many banners in efforts to restructure culture. New synonyms appear every day for the same old cast of deceptions. Nevertheless, the struggle is always with all "arguments and every pretension that sets itself up against the knowledge of God."[9]

The work of the trowel is the never-ending task of apologetics, of skillful presentation of Christian truth. "Contend[ing] for the faith that was once for all entrusted to the saints."[10] The responsibility certainly has its very real costs.

One of the earliest Christian apologists, Tertullian knew well and personally the dangers of this approach. Writing of the cost, the opposition, and the ultimate importance of speaking out, Tertullian said, "The blood of the martyrs is the seed of the church."

Today death often comes in different forms than Tertullian witnessed in the Colosseum in Rome—but it still comes. Georgetown University Professor James V. Schall said of the contemporary battle: "The cruelest form of death, I have no doubt, is not physical death. Rather it is that public death which comes from the killing of ideas about God, about natural law, about the real dimensions of what loving means. It comes from not talking about good and evil, from being too modest even to bring them forth."[11]

In contrast, we believe in resurrection. The walls of civility are going up again!

CHAPTER 4

HOW COME YOU'RE THE TARGET?

CRESTVIEW IS in the panhandle section of Florida. In the center of town is a lovely wooded area lined with benches and picnic tables. Triangle Park, a popular spot many people drive past daily, is a natural choice for an expression of community conviction.

Donnie Cadenhead is the pastor of Victorious Life Worship Center. He and the congregation wanted to make an unusual and dramatic statement of their faith during Easter week 1994.

They approached the city council with a request to display three large crosses in Triangle Park to symbolize the passion and death of Christ.

The city council wasn't unsympathetic but were concerned about erecting religious objects on public property. They worried about violating the "separation of church and state" because the issue seemed to be controversial. During the meeting, city officials requested Pastor Cadenhead contact the ACLJ for guidance on the legalities of a Christian display in a public park.

The problem for Pastor Cadenhead and the Victorious Life Worship Center wasn't a hostile city government or contemptuous local attorneys. The issue was confusion over state law and *concern for being attacked by outside groups.* The issue was the result of decades of misinformation by many of our adversaries.

Jay notes that increasingly the ACLJ is being asked by city governments to offer assistance when religious issues arise. In Crestview, the city attorney was concerned that groups like the ACLU would leap on the situation and create significant problems for the city. Jay knew the value and importance of Christian displays in public parks. Depicting Jesus on a cross was a natural and normal statement of the meaning of the season. Consequently, he went to Crestview and appeared before the city council.

Because the ACLJ had seen tremendous courtroom success in opening public places and parks to Christian symbols, Jay was armed with a massive amount of material on the subject. His job was to help the city attorney determine how to advise the council. Staff lawyers with the ACLJ national office began preparing the necessary legal memorandums.

When Jay walked into the council's chamber room he noticed emblazoned on the wall "In God We Trust." Every seat in the chamber was packed with youth groups and members of local churches. Dozens of people stood in the hallways. A good omen, indeed! For the next forty minutes Jay discussed how the law applied to the display of crosses in public parks.

The ACLJ's public handbook, *Knowing Your Rights,* details the thrust of Jay's presentation in a form that any citizen can use in a similar situation. As a matter of law, the Supreme Court has never said that private citizens can be barred from setting up nativity displays or any other scene of a religious nature. In fact the Supreme Court recently made it clear that religious expression in a public place like Triangle Park is protected by the First Amendment.

The easiest way to understand the legal issues is to think of an Easter or Christmas display as a message to fellow citizens. Clearly, the government cannot meddle with your message. The Supreme Court has stated, "If there is any fixed star in our constitutional constellation, it is that no official, high or petty, can prescribe what shall be orthodox in politics, nationalism, religion, or other matters of opinion or force citizens to confess by word or act their faith therein."[1] Park authorities or officials cannot determine for you what expression is appropriate in your private display.

At the end of Jay's presentation, the city council unanimously approved the church's display of crosses.

Pastor Cadenhead later wrote:

Dear Brother Jay,

Enclosed are the articles written concerning our live crucifix in Crestview, Florida.

We had two local television stations do lead stories concerning the scenes and Bennett Luke used the city hall film and the crucifix to do a program we were on.

We estimated between 30,000 to 50,000 cars went by the display. We believe as many as 100,000 people saw it. We had over 3,000 people actually stop and walk into the park.

Our church had over 30 first-time visitors this past Sunday.

We thank God, Jay Sekulow, and David Etheriedge for the victory.

But the larger question is, Why all the ruckus? Why do good people have such a struggle in a land that once guaranteed everyone free access to all forms of public expression?

The New Climate

The term *religious cleansing* is an accurate and effective way of expressing the current hostility and bigotry toward all civic expressions of religion. Rather than use the physical extermination methods of the Bosnian Serbs, these religious cleansers use political and legal means of containment. They are America's new anti-faith bigots.

How do they take aim at you?

Religious people are often described with pejorative language—*intolerant, extremist, fundamentalists, zealots, fanatics.* The term *fundamentalist* is often used for strategic reasons. As John Green, professor of political science at the

University of Akron, observed, the word is now synonymous with "nasty, narrow-minded hayseed, poorly educated and anti-intellectual." What right-thinking person would want such clods to have a vital role in public affairs and politics?

The media have been used to demean believers. Movies and television programs portray religious people, and especially Christians, as bungling morons; naive, ill-equipped counselors; or con men ready to pounce on innocent victims. Newspeople often skillfully slant stories. A *Washington Post* news article described Christians as "poor, uneducated and easy to command." Cartoonists take cheap shots as well. Pat Oliphant recently depicted Christians as rats, dragging the Republican party into the "Fundamentalist Christian Mission" in order to save it.

The situation has become bad enough that journalists can no longer overlook the implications of their own conduct. Political reporter Laurence Barrett of *Time* recently wrote in the *Columbia Journalism Review,* "Though the [religious] movement has significant internal differences, we tend to depict it as monolithic." Barrett argued that this often happens because few journalists are religious followers themselves. "It's an easy call to recognize that we need a broad sensitivity check . . . whatever we think of its agenda, we must get ourselves to church, if only as observers."[2]

Barrett is correct. Such journalistic inaccuracies and attacks have helped create the new climate of religious intolerance in American life. Nowhere does the problem become more explosively obvious than in politics. When people of religious conviction express political concern, they are immediately labeled as the religious right, with the inference of demagoguery.

Aiming at the Kids

What practical shape does the attack take? Kids have been a major target in the last several decades. Often without realizing their complicity, leaders in the education establishment have been effectively enlisted in the assault. Secularists have succeeded in putting Christians on the defensive and effectively censoring religious expression and the use of the Bible.

Here are some typical examples.

- In Manassas, Virginia, ten-year-old Audrey Pearson began taking her Bible with her to help pass the time on her hour-long bus ride to school. The principal said she could not bring her Bible to school because of church/state separation. Audrey's family did not tolerate this distorted interpretation of the U.S. Constitution. They had to press the issue to secure her right to bring her Bible on the bus.
- A fourth-grade girl in Massachusetts put crosses in an art project. A teacher told the student she couldn't do so. The matter was challenged, and religious freedoms had to be explained to the teacher. She apologized.
- An Omaha, Nebraska, fifth grader was told he must take his Bible home after he read from it during a free-reading period. When the student's father asked the principal if the school library contained a Bible, he admitted it did.

> But, the principal said, that Bible was for reference use by adults only.

Get the picture?

Don't these examples sound strangely like the political shape secularism took earlier in this century? Marxist Russia showed how devastating it can be when politicians use the language of opposites, saying one thing that means another. There the government closed churches in the name of religious liberty. How different is this current attack in America in the name of "freedom" from what was promoted by the state in the Communist Soviet Union in the name of—yes, you got it—"religious freedom"? Like a very bad joke, haven't we heard this one before?

Is Conviction a Political Sin?

To the surprise of many, President Clinton said at a recent prayer breakfast, "The people of faith in this country ought to be able to say that religion shapes their approach to public debate without someone saying, 'Oh, you're just being a right-winger.'" The ACLJ couldn't agree more.

The problem has been the religious cleansers operate under the guise of civil liberty and the U.S. Constitution, contending in the political arena and the courts that the so-called separation of church and state means that religious beliefs, values, and practices should be barred from the public square.

Religious people can sit in their homes and places of worship and discuss political, moral, and social issues, and they can vote their consciences. But if they move beyond these borders and step into city hall, or the courts, or the public schools, or virtually any other community arena, they become trespassers, violators to be hurled back into the private sphere where their ideas cannot affect, or even threaten to affect, anyone but themselves.

Clinton is right. "The environment in which we operate is entirely too secular." Contrary to what secularists want us to believe, President Clinton went on to say, "Freedom of religion doesn't mean that those of us who have faith shouldn't frankly admit that we are animated by that faith, that we try to live by it—and that it does affect what we feel, what we think, and what we do."[3]

Again, Clinton is right. We do need "a new ethic of personal and family and community responsibility in this country that should unite people." Keith has written forcibly, "That ethic cannot come from secularism, which has no adequate moral base from which to draw. It must come from a religious orientation that clearly understands what Clinton referred to as 'self-evidently true: you cannot change somebody's life from the outside in unless there is also some change from the inside out.' People of faith know that the power for internal change comes from a relationship with God."[4]

President Clinton is correct in his assessment of the importance of the influence of faithful people. The history of this country has well demonstrated that religious people have always proven to be an asset to national life. If their message is censored out of the marketplace, the country loses. The real issue is backing up the rhetoric with pro-liberty, pro-life, and pro-family public policy, which the president failed to do.

The work of the ACLJ has made Christians harder targets

to hit today than they were three decades ago. Jay reports, "We have seen efforts to stop Christian students from evangelizing in or outside their public schools shut down. We have seen city councils once again permit nativity scenes to be displayed on public property. We have seen religious intolerance curtailed, free speech protected, the rights of pro-life advocates upheld, and religious expression encouraged."

Changing the Climate

One never knows where and when the battle will begin again. Marietta Bell was simply going about her business as a successful real estate agent when she ran into the Arizona Fair Housing Authority. Marietta always used the fish, an ancient Christian symbol, on her real estate advertisements because she wanted her customers to know where she stood and what they could expect from her services. Her real estate advertisements reflected the principles Bell lives by.

Unexpectedly and unfortunately, the attorney general of Arizona took a different view of freedom and liberty. The Arizona Fair Housing Authority published a politically correct "Advertising Word and Phrase List" that outlawed some of Marietta's favorite ways to identify herself. The words were "unacceptable" and could only be used with "caution." Christian, church, and religious references were on the hit list. Use of these words was now illegal.

Marietta Bell was violating the law by using the fish symbol in ads and on her business card! Government officials informed her that further use of such material would result in legal action. Her Christian witness had become a criminal offense.

Marietta contacted the ACLJ, and we immediately initiated litigation on her behalf, naming the attorney general of Arizona as the defendant. A lawsuit was filed in federal court alleging that Marietta's freedom of speech and free exercise of religion had been violated. She was not backing down.

As the case approached a trial date, the attorney general blinked and agreed to settle. On February 9, 1995, the United States District Judge reviewed the settlement and allowed the case to stand. The agreement read in part: "Defendant Woods agrees that use of Christian religious symbols, including without limitation, the 'icthus' or 'fish,' in her real estate advertising in newspaper, business card, and flyers is not a violation of . . . the Arizona Fair Housing Word List." Marietta Bell stood up for her rights and won!

Don't Discount the Pogo Factor

Remember that famous line in the comic strip when Pogo comments on the state of affairs in the country? He concludes, "We have seen the enemy and he is us!"

Before the Christian community concludes that the problem is entirely "them," we must also recognize the "us" dimension. The "Chicken Little syndrome" has been a major problem for Christians and churches for more than two decades. The sudden onslaught of attacks on religious liberty sent many believers running for shelter before a piece of the sky smashed them too. A defeatist mentality and a retreat mindset made these naysayers equally a part of the problem. Accustomed to two centuries of openness, the sudden chill in the religious climate caused many to turn tail without confrontation. Taking flight makes us part of the problem.

It is time to regain our common Christian memory. Christians historically have gone from martyrdom in coliseums to bringing about the conversion of nations. Following in the footsteps of the Savior, we are the people who form a human bridge between heaven and earth, holding the sky up! Saint Augustine reminded us that we are first and foremost citizens of "the City of God," transformers of the secular city into a place of light and hope.

The staff of the ACLJ believes we are privileged to live in an exciting age of challenge. Rather than living in a "post-Christian" period, we are in a "pre-Christian" phase of history, offering us the challenge to bring conversion to the generation both around and behind us. Failure to accept this mission makes us the enemy.

Putting on the Boxing Gloves

The enemy is defeatable! We simply have to dare to get into the war. Jay put on the gloves in the *Bray v. Alexandria Women's Health Clinic* case. Planned Parenthood and the National Organization of Women attempted to use the Ku Klux Klan Act of 1871 to justify the harassment dished out on pro-life demonstrators. The National Organization of Women (NOW) attempted to argue that opposition to abortion was discrimination against women. On that basis, they evoked the Klan act aimed at stopping racist groups engaged in terrorist activities, but used it to suppress pro-life free speech.

Jay forcefully argued to the U.S. Supreme Court that

NOW's position was not only a misapplication of the law but a clear violation of the First Amendment. Keith served as co-counsel. The justices heard the *Bray* argument and agreed with Jay's position. This misapplication of the law was stopped. The battle was fought and won.

For his representation in this case, the National Religious Broadcasters Board of Directors award was given to Jay on January 29, 1994. At that time Keith said, "Jay is the Thurgood Marshall of our movement." The award and comment were simply affirmations of what follows when Christians stand up in the fray and fight.

Yes, there are barbarians at the gate and Trojan horses in the city. The statistical results of the attack are alarming. Nevertheless, the tide is turning, and the battle is being won.

PART 2

THE BATTLE ZONE

CHAPTER 5

RESTORING THE CHRISTIAN VOICE

IN WAR, battle zones shift and change. Confrontations develop as enemy forces move unexpectedly across the terrain. Armies must be prepared lest a seemingly minor skirmish become the center of a major encounter. Similarly, some of the most important breakthroughs in the religious liberties battle in recent years have been the result of alert citizens recognizing the denial of their rights as a call to arms. Their refusal to retreat set the stage for new victories in the struggle to restore the Christian voice.

Nowhere is the strife more significant and far-reaching than in the struggle to recover religious speech in the marketplace. For three decades, Christian witness has been under attack in the name of the law of the land. The 1962 prayer decision of the Supreme Court started a monumental landslide burying religious freedom. Other attacks came in rapid succession.

- In a 1965 case, the Court let stand a ruling that said that it was unconstitutional for a student to pray out loud before eating his lunch.
- In a Colorado case, a teacher was told that he could not leave the Bible he was reading during a free period on his desk in public view.
- The display of the Ten Commandments in public schools was ruled illegal in 1980.
- An Alabama law allowing students to have a moment of silence was ruled unconstitutional in 1980 because of the possibility that a teacher might be suggesting prayer. Meditation was acceptable, but prayer was illegal.
- In 1987, the Supreme Court ruled that public schools could not require teachers to teach the biblical account of creation along with evolution.

Today, people of faith are no longer on the defense. What turned the tides?

The Courage to Confront

A major turning point came with the state of New York's attempt to silence a small congregation bent on making a big witness. Lamb's Chapel was a nondenominational church in upstate New York trying to reach the community by offering help for the entire family. James Dobson's *Turn Your Heart Toward "Home"* was selected for screening because of its important message for young families. The high school routinely opened the auditorium to all local groups promoting the welfare of the community, so the church's application was totally in order. Strangely enough, this modest little Christian church's petition was not only rejected but attacked by the state of New York with a vengeance.

The state's position was simple. Because the film was religious, it was "obviously" a threat to public order. Citizens had to be protected against such intrusions into their freedom!

The Long Island village of Center Moriches seems to be an unlikely place to draw a line in the sand. This quiet residential community was founded in 1700 in the heavily wooded forests of the Great South Bay. The town was more pastoral than pugilistic. When John Steigerwald and Allen Snapp moved there in 1988, their only objective was to spread the gospel of peace. The young graduates from Christ for the Nations Bible College in nearby Stonybrook were deeply committed to developing the ministry of a small evangelical congregation founded five years earlier.

With only sixty members, Lamb's Chapel was a church of young middle-class families concerned for increased fellowship and emotional connectedness. Worship services were held in a rented sanctuary on Sunday afternoons. The congregation emphasized personal relationships more than church programs. Lamb's Chapel was a warm, caring gathering of enthusiastic young Christians. They wanted to attract families and help them increase their capacity to be effective parents. James Dobson's film was an excellent vehicle for providing unchurched, struggling young families with vital information.

Because the Center Moriches School District rented school facilities to many community organizations, the pastor wrote for permission to rent the school's auditorium for five successive Wednesday nights. He received a vague response indicating "suspicion" because the film's contents seemed to be religious. After a series of exchanges, the district refused to rent because the use appeared to be church-related.

Although advised that the church was the victim of unconstitutional discrimination against religious speech, the church struggled with the advisability of a lawsuit. Following the tragic death of two small children in the congregation, nerves were frayed and emotions were raw. The elders and deacons weren't sure if the church was up to a court battle.

Finally, church leaders felt it was essential to take a bold stand. Two lower federal courts heard the case but sided with the school district's policy. At that point, Lamb's Chapel turned to the ACLJ, and chief counsel Jay Sekulow took the case. On February 24, 1993, the lawsuit reached the Supreme Court for review. In a very unusual turn of events, the American Civil Liberties Union, the Union of American Hebrew Congregations, and the People for the American Way stood with the church in amicus briefs. Their consensus was that the use of public properties posed no possibility of government entanglement with religion or the church. In contrast, New York State's Attorney General Robert Abrams argued that religion has no value except to the people who believe it.

The Showdown at the Top

The final confrontation in the highest court in the land proved to be a fascinating microcosm of what was happening across the land. The attorneys for the school district made their secular assault on the religious establishment plain and clear. Attorney for the district John Hoefling forcefully repeated the school policy to deny access to all religious organizations and persons even though atheists, anti-religious activists, Communists, and secularists could rent the school's facilities. Hoefling insisted that numerous atheists could refute religion and Christian faith in meetings on this public property but that the doors would be closed to anyone presenting a Christian defense.

The dismay of the justices quickly became clear. Justices Sandra Day O'Connor and Clarence Thomas asked clarifying questions that further exposed how extreme the district's position truly was. Hoefling maintained that both New York law and the U.S. Constitution mandated that "the premises would not be used for religious purposes."[1] Justices continued to question Hoefling. Would the district allow people to come in urging adoption of a lifestyle "secularly inspired but not religiously inspired"? Without hesitancy, the attorney said yes. Again the justices probed, asking if advocating a lifestyle based on religious values would be allowed. Hoefling made it clear such a presentation would not be allowed.

The Court asked, "If you had a Communist group that wanted to address the subject of family values and they thought there was a value in not having children waste their time going to Sunday school or church and therefore they had a point of view that was definitely antireligion, they would be permitted, under your policy, to discuss family values in that context?" The attorney's answer was emphatically affirmative.[2] Lest we appear to be vilifying attorney Hoefling, the context of his viewpoint must be made clear. In addition to presenting the district's policy, he was merely articulating the stance of the American educational establishment.

Allen Snapp, assistant pastor at Lamb's Chapel, had repeatedly encountered a hostile attitude on the part of the leadership of Center Moriches Union School District well before the legal showdown. A student from Lamb's Chapel sought permission for an after-school Bible club. Though rebuffed, the sophomore had told the principal that the 1990 *Westside Community Schools v. Mergens* case meant that the school couldn't deny access to the students. In turn, the principal demanded a list of the students in the Bible club and wanted to know who worshiped at Lamb's Chapel. Pastor Snapp confronted the principal about undue and unusual surveillance. The principal's stated view was that Lamb's Chapel was a source of trouble for the school system. Nevertheless, Allen Snapp was not afraid to stand his ground. The result changed the shape of school/church relationships.[3]

Implications for the Future

By the time the battle in the Supreme Court was finished, the hostility Pastors Snapp and Steigerwald experienced was exposed to daylight. Jay argued at the Supreme Court that "The Communists are in, the atheists are in, the agnostics are in, but religion's out because we don't like their viewpoint."[4]

But here's the rest of the story! The belligerence of state and local officials was turned back because of the courage of two pastors and their congregation and because of the availability of the ACLJ. The Supreme Court unanimously determined that speech restrictions, religious or otherwise, are unconstitutional, even in a nonpublic forum. The state and district's antagonism to Lamb's Chapel was ruled completely out of order.

The Supreme Court made it abundantly clear "there is a crucial difference between *government* speech endorsing religion, which the Establishment Clause forbids, and *private* speech endorsing religion, which the Free Speech and Free Exercise Clauses protect."[5] Confusion over this distinction had led to many instances of antagonism toward religious groups, particularly Christian groups, on the part of local, state, and national agencies.

Unfortunately, some government officials have not yet fully grasped the reality of this decision and continue to exhibit animosity toward religious speakers. Nevertheless, government officials cannot exclude speakers or exhibit viewpoint discrimination by denying equal access to public property.

Actually, this position was clearly established a decade earlier. In January 1977, the University of Missouri refused to allow Cornerstone, a Christian group, access to a meeting room on campus. More than one hundred groups were registered and accepted as bona fide student organizations. The university, however, singled out the kids of Cornerstone because their meetings included Bible reading and an atmosphere of worship. The school's regulations forbade use of buildings and grounds for such purposes by students and nonstudents.

Once again courageous students stood their ground. Cornerstone challenged the constitutionality of such treatment. The battle was on, and this case also ended up in the Supreme Court.

The Law of the land held that religious discussion and worship "are forms of speech and association protected by the First Amendment."[6] Cornerstone's battle made two principles clear. First, religious worship and teaching are protected under the Free Speech Clause of the First Amendment. Second, there is no conflict with separation of church and state when religious meetings are given the right of assembly.

The government can't muzzle the church or those who bear witness to their faith.

The Consequences of Silence

The Lamb's Chapel case revealed another significant result of past decades of hostility to the Christian enterprise. During the arguments, Jay zeroed in on the key issue. The school district was intentionally trying to suppress a religious viewpoint! He noted that precisely because the subject matter was theological the state was forbidden by the U.S. Constitution from intervening or stifling any presentation or discussion of the subject.

Justice Antonin Scalia leaned over the lofty wooden bench and asked the opposing attorney to explain the rationale and reasoning behind the rejection of the church's rental request. The attorney stammered and waffled, trying to express the school board's concern for the greater good of the public.

Justice Scalia read the attorney general of New York's statement that religious advocacy yields a benefit only to believers. The judge noted that he had grown up in New York State and there was once a tax exemption for religious property. "Is that still there?" he asked the attorney.

"Well, your Honor . . . " Mr. Hoefling struggled for words.

Justice Scalia bore down. "You see, it used to be thought that religion . . . it didn't matter what religion . . . but the code of morality that always went with it, was thought to result in what was called a God-fearing person, that might be less likely to mug me and rape my sister. That apparently is not the view of New York anymore."

The New York assistant attorney general struggled to find some adequate response. "Well, I'm not sure that . . . that's . . . that . . . "

With a sly grin on his face, Justice Scalia asked almost sarcastically, "Has this new regime worked very well?" The courtroom broke out in laughter.

The answer to the justice's question is found in every section of American life. President Ronald Reagan's secretary of education William Bennett painted a vivid response in *The Index of Leading Cultural Indicators.* Since 1960 America's population increased by 41 percent, domestic products nearly tripled, and social spending at all levels of government rose from $142.73 billion to $787 billion.

During the same period, violent crime increased 560 percent, illegitimate births rose 400 percent, divorces quadrupled, the number of children living in single-parent homes tripled, and teenage suicides increased more than 200 percent. High school SAT scores dropped an average of 75 points![7]

Look at the loss of the moral anchor that religion provides from another angle. In 1940 school teachers identified the top problems in the classroom as talking out of turn, chewing gum, making noise, running in the hall, cutting in line, dress-code infractions, and littering. In 1990 teachers had a very different list. Today's problems are drugs, alcohol abuse, pregnancy, suicide, rape, robbery, and assault.

How do we stack up with the other industrialized countries of the world? According to William Bennett, "We are at or near the top in rates of abortions, divorces, and unwed births. We lead the industrialized world in murder, rape, and violent crime. And in elementary and secondary education, we are at or near the bottom in achievement scores.[8]

If Justice Scalia had asked the current generation of fifteen- to twenty-four-year-olds (the group raised in the new environment, popularly called Generation X) to answer his question, "Has this new regime worked very well?" they would have been even less encouraging. Each day of the week this age group can expect:

13 of their peers to commit suicide

16 to be murdered

90 to be assigned to a foster home

2,200 to drop out of school

3,610 to be assaulted

80 to be raped

630 to be robbed

500 to start using drugs

1,000 to become mothers[9]

Every day.

The answer to Justice Scalia's question is painfully obvious. *No,* the new regime is not working. And we haven't even inquired about the full extent of the loss of life from the new philosophy.

The legal and political crackdown on the church's voice and religious influence has been a disaster.

The New Day

We are now at a different place. Because a few people exhibited significant stamina, American Christians are once again in a new and open environment. In their unanimous decision, the Court said that a Christian organization's confronting contemporary issues from a biblical perspective cannot be excluded from access to property the government makes available to other organizations. Christians are not second-class citizens!

Knowing Your Rights: Taking Back Our Religious Liberties: A Handbook was prepared by Jay Sekulow for distribution through the Christian Broadcasting Network. The full details of the implications are spelled out for your use in those pages. In summary, here is the ground on which you stand.

- In many communities, local school facilities are the

town halls of the community. Many non-Christians feel more comfortable going to such a place rather than a church to hear discussions of contemporary issues. Christians have a right to use this forum. Every government agency, from school boards to city councils that create policy, must allow Christians utilization of these facilities if others are permitted to use them.

- Openness doesn't apply only to churches. Even parachurch organizations can hold evangelistic crusades in school auditoriums. The decision in favor of Lamb's Chapel applies to any government facility that has been opened for use by the public.
- The government cannot selectively determine what views will be presented or discussed. Family issues, baccalaureate services for students, evangelistic events, and discussions of a variety of contemporary issues by Christians cannot be prohibited in the marketplace.

The Ripple Effect

Quick and confrontational action by Christians will result in stopping shutdowns. A good example is Phyllis Mulazzi and her insistence on the public library allowing her right of access.

The Mulazzi family and their three children are members of the Faith of God Word Ministry in Farmingville, New York. Phyllis's church has been a vital force in her life and spiritual development. When her brother was terribly scarred in a fire, the family laid on hands and he was totally healed. Similar experiences had completely transformed Phyllis's faith and life.

The family church invited contemporary Christian musician Phil Driscoll to perform. The concert was an opportunity to make contact with the secular community and needed advertisement in places where outsiders would see the invitation.

Remembering the community bulletin board in the Sachem Public Library, Phyllis took a second look. She found many notices, including a children's theater event, the Thirteenth Annual Chamber Music Festival, a sandcastle contest, auditions for *The Nutcracker,* and a posting for the Summer Cultural Arts Concert. But the library officials told her she could not use the bulletin board. Her poster had a picture of Driscoll with the heading, "CAMP MEETING '94 SPIRIT OF REVIVAL." Librarians said the notice was simply "too religious." If she would remove the word *revival,* the poster could go up. Phyllis told the officials their refusal was discriminatory. The official said flatly, "We cannot inundate the public with religion."

Phyllis was shocked. She remembers thinking, *How can they deny me? I'm a citizen.* For the first time in her life Phyllis felt like her personal rights were stripped away.

Even more significant, Phyllis realized Jesus Christ was being denied. Her savior and healer was too important for her to allow the library's slight to stand.

After further inquiry the library advisory board of trustees made a final decision that the poster was "not appropriate for a library, because it was too religious." Phyllis returned home in despair.

But Phyllis's husband had been very active in the Christian Coalition and a member of the ACLJ. The family had been members of the 700 Club for years. They naturally called Virginia Beach for help.

Diligent staffers noted that her request came in on July 18, 1994, and the concert was July 23. No time to waste! The wheels began to turn immediately. The next day the ACLJ sent a letter to the Sachem Public Library's attorney in Northfork, New York, via Federal Express. The letter made it clear that a demand was being made on behalf of Phyllis to require the library to do "whatever was necessary to ensure that officials of the library do not continue to violate Phyllis's constitutional rights to freedom of speech, freedom of press, and freedom of association." The eight-page letter set forth the facts of the case and the relevant law.

Because Sachem Public Library opened its bulletin board to the community, it had created a public forum. The library authority was taking the position that religious speech was somehow entitled to second-class treatment and that the so-called separation of church and state would empower the authority to censor the poster from display. The letter from the ACLJ makes it clear that "above all else, the First Amendment means that government has no power to restrict expression because of its message, its idea, its subject matter, or its contents . . . the essence of this forbidden censorship is content control."

The ACLJ, on behalf of Phyllis Mulazzi, sent a straightforward demand to the library trustees. "It is imperative that the Sachem Public Library discontinue their interference with Phyllis Mulazzi's right to use the bulletin board on equal basis with other groups of the community. If these violations continue and she is prevented from advertising this event, we will inform our client of her right to seek appropriate redress in federal district court." The Sachem library was given one day to respond.

We did not intend to be harsh, but we believe the gospel message is a life-or-death matter. We get dozens of calls each week from people in unjust situations similar to what Phyllis Mulazzi faced. Consequently, we must take an aggressive stance when it comes to the denial of the proclamation of the gospel.

The day after the receipt of ACLJ's letter, on July 20, 1994, Douglas K. McNally, the attorney for the library's trustees wrote, "I have forwarded a copy of your letter to the director of the library. The library staff will contact Mrs. Mulazzi today and advise her that her flyer may be immediately posted on the library's public bulletin board."

When the librarian called, her attitude had so completely changed that Phyllis didn't recognize the voice. The lady confessed that no one had ever challenged their position and that she didn't realize rights were being violated. Interestingly enough, the librarian mused that there were books on God in the library so why not a poster on religion?

As Phyllis looks back on the incident, she reflects, "People must not be afraid to stand up for what they believe. If they don't, our rights will soon be taken away from us. Even if we have to go on trial, God will take care of us."

Phyllis Mulazzi's willingness to stand up for her rights had opened the door for all other Christian groups in her community. The Lord provided a victory that sent a message to all Christians. We must utilize the public forum whether it be bulletin boards, schools, or auditoriums to proclaim the message of Jesus Christ.

Moving Out

It is time for Christians to go on the offensive and have our voices heard. We must utilize the rights obtained from the Supreme Court decisions. Hundreds of government policy manuals still prohibit religious groups from using facilities open to the larger community. We must aggressively confront these situations and demand change.

The procedure to gain access to any public facility is straightforward.

1. You must fill out an application form available through the local government. Be forthright in stating your purposes.
2. If you are denied access, ask local authorities if they are familiar with the Lamb's Chapel case. If they are not, the ACLJ will be glad to send a clarification letter on your behalf.
3. If you are still denied, the ACLJ can send a demand letter on your behalf. Generally the demand letter brings immediate resolution of the problem.
4. Obstinacy beyond this point calls for appeal to federal court to obtain an injunction.

The fruits of this approach are now being seen across America. When people like Pastors Steigerwald and Snapp and citizens like Phyllis Mulazzi persevere, the ACLJ is able to demonstrate that Christianity can go head to head with hostility and discrimination and demonstrate its intellectual and practical superiority.

CHAPTER 6

CENSORSHIP ON CAMPUS

THE SEVENTEEN-YEAR-OLD BOY looked like any other kid, an unlikely candidate for espionage or illegal activity. He quickly edged past his peers, hurrying toward his friend and confidant. The two students made eye contact as soon as they left their opposite classrooms. Time between classes was short, and the hall monitors were always watching.

Contact had to be quick and unnoticed. They wandered toward each other with an intended air of casualness. Unaware, other students hurried down the narrow halls toward their assigned classrooms for the next period. As the two teens passed, a note was slipped between them. The second boy quickly headed for his classroom with the note wadded in his hand. Unfortunately, he had already been observed.

The clandestine information was quickly confiscated and passed to the head of the school. Before the end of the next period, the young lad was called into the office to explain his deviant behavior. He listened in dread as the principal read the secret note.

The administrator laid the issues out clearly. Everything was now known. The plot was exposed. The student had invited his friend to an after-school Christian gathering. The authorities were very upset. For this subversive behavior, the student was immediately suspended. He was charged with a very serious offense . . . *possession of Christian materials.*

Sound like a story from Russia? Communist China? Cuba? The secret police of Saddam Hussein catching a missionary in Iraq? Unfortunately, no. On November 21, 1989, the drama unfolded in Henderson High School near Atlanta, Georgia. The student's name was Scott McDaniel. He was seen handing a note to his friend Matt Hinton in the hallway as classes changed. Scott informed Matt of an off-campus meeting of the officers of the Fellowship of Christian Athletes. When the assistant principal intercepted the note, Scott was suspended for three days. Matt was threatened with suspension.

Earlier in the day, Matt had been warned to put a jacket over a Christian T-shirt. The principal told Matt's father, Bill Hinton, that if Matt or any student brought a Bible to school or wore a religious T-shirt or button, further suspension would follow. Discipline was noted on the boy's school records with the actual charge listed as "suspension for possession of Christian material."

Notice was served that the Fellowship of Christian Athletes could not meet on campus or participate in any school-related activities. They would not be allowed to march in the homecoming parade or be in the school yearbook—unless the word *Christian* was deleted.

The ultimate irony is what was happening across the world at essentially the same time—in Russia. Quite the opposite was unfolding in the country that had for nearly a century been the center of persecution of Christians. In an update on changes in the Soviet Union, *USA Today* reported that in Russia all 65,000 public school principals, teachers, and administrators were receiving training on biblically based ethics. Russian public school teacher Natasha Popova told the paper that she now teaches her students, "Jesus Christ is God's son and he died for our sins. . . . He is alive today and can be our best friend." Olga Melnikova, a Russian assistant principal, said, "For a short period—seventy-four years—we lost it all. The Bible is now part of normal education." English teacher Natasha Pimenova commented, "We're desperate for faith. Faith is freedom and Stalin was afraid of freedom. He must be rolling over in his grave."[1]

What the Soviets fought so hard to recover and enjoy had been summarily ripped away in America by school administrators bent on eradicating religious presence from our country's school systems.

Fortunately, Scott's and Matt's parents refused to take the abuse and stood behind their sons. Jay Sekulow and his associates moved quickly to combat the hostility and turn back this flagrant violation of the First Amendment. A demand letter was sent to the school, and administrators retreated. The boys were reinstated and their records cleared. The school stopped harassing students for bringing Bibles and tracts and wearing Christian T-shirts to school.

Standing Behind Our Kids

No arena is more important, with greater long-range significance, than the struggle for the minds and attitudes of the young. The outcome will determine the shape of tomorrow. We cannot stand back and allow our youth to be taught fear of witnessing to their faith. Kids must not think believing in Christ turns them into second-rate teens.

You need to know we don't have to live with the problems Scott and Matt faced. A new beginning was established in 1990 when Bridget Mergens took her case to the Supreme Court and won. The battle began when Bridget started a Bible club on her high school campus in Omaha, Nebraska. The Westside Community Board of Education viewed her actions as religious intrusion into their secularized environment.

In 1984, seventeen-year-old Bridget Mergens and her friends wanted to start a Bible club on the campus of Omaha's Westside High School to meet once a week for an hour. Not even seeking the endorsement of the school, Bridget, as a Christian, simply wanted the same privilege accorded other groups.

Appealing to the old "separation of church and state" argument, the principal vetoed the Bible club. Bridget persevered and appealed to both the assistant school superintendent and finally the school board. In each instance, they also said no.

When Bridget's struggle ended up in court, a district judge in Omaha seized upon a part of the Equal Access Act in a ludicrous attempt to justify the school's rejection of the religious organization. The act actually requires equal access to facilities if the school allows noncurriculum-related groups use of properties. The judge decided the Bible club wasn't curriculum-related. Of course, approximately thirty of the thirty-five clubs at Westside weren't curriculum related; at the very least, by his definition the chess club and the scuba club shouldn't have qualified!

In an age when students go through metal detectors before entering school, one would think the Bible would be considered something less than an undesirable "weapon" in the classroom. The Westside board's efforts to ban the club proved illegal when Jay took over the case.

The Students' Bill of Rights

By the time Bridget's battle was won, the Supreme Court had clearly affirmed and upheld the students' rights to speak and express their convictions on the campus. The *Westside Community Board of Education v. Mergens* decision interpreted the Congressional Equal Access Act of 1984 as ensuring high school students are not discriminated against in the public schools because of religious beliefs. The Court held that Bible clubs and prayer groups *can* assemble on public school properties.

The ruling clearly meant that public secondary schools

receiving federal funds and allowing noncurriculum-related clubs to meet on campus must also allow Bible clubs and prayer groups to meet on campus during noninstructional time. Justice O'Connor clarified the issue in her ruling by stating, "If a State refused to let religious groups use facilities open to others, then it would demonstrate not neutrality but *hostility* toward religion."[2]

Almost all public secondary schools receive federal funds. Simply put, if a school has clubs that are not a part of a regular class or directly related to a school class, the school must allow the Bible club the same privileges. If the school allows service clubs such as Interact and 4-H, it must allow religious groups.

The Supreme Court decision was the answer to the prayers of multitudes of God's people across our nation. The 8-1 decision was also a clear message to the country that the time was ripe for action. Students *can* share the gospel with their peers without school or government interruption. Today the key ingredient in change is the citizen on the local firing line demanding that all government agencies comply with the law of the land.

Once a Supreme Court ruling is made, it is binding on all lower courts, federal and state. In this instance, the Court's position means the idea of "separation of church and state" cannot keep religion out of the public school. As a matter of fact, the U.S. Constitution never uses such a phrase. Nowhere in the notes of the Constitutional Convention was the idea of separation of church and state recorded. The framers of our republic never envisioned hostility of the state toward religious expression.

The Constitution says, "Congress shall make no law respecting an establishment of religion, or prohibiting the free exercise thereof." The Constitution in no way mandated the exclusion of religion from public schools or for that matter the public square. While school-sponsored religious activity *was* prohibited, free exercise and free speech are our rights under the Constitution. The school cannot propose or promote a state religion, but it also cannot block religious speech or expression. Promoting and prohibiting are worlds apart!

Examples of Victory

The next step is for courageous students to demand their rights. Melissa Graham is an example of the difference one person can make. Near the end of 1994, she contacted the ACLJ offices for help.

Melissa and her friends formed the Intercessors Christian Club at Northwest High School in Justin, Texas. She and her friends made a clear Christian witness on the campus and prayed for the well-being of the school. They wanted their friends to know Jesus Christ as Lord. Intercessors Christian Club attempted to reach out to their peers.

Trouble began when Melissa tried to use the school bulletin board. School administrators would allow her to advertise meeting times and places but refused to allow signs with reference to "God" or "Jesus." Administration fell back on the hackneyed excuse that blatant religious references violated "separation of church and state." The battle was on! Melissa called the ACLJ.

Once we received Melissa's urgent request, we contacted our Phoenix, Arizona, offices and asked them to help. They sent a demand letter to school officials clarifying that the *Mergens* decision meant that "official recognition allows student clubs to be part of the student activities program and carries with it access to the school newspaper, bulletin boards, public address system, and the annual club fair." Melissa and her friends had the right to be an integral part of the campus life of their school and must be allowed to be an influence on the student body at Northwest High School.

We wrote the high school that refusing equal treatment with other noncurriculum clubs meeting on campus relegates those students to the position of second-class citizens. Our letter made it clear that school officials do not automatically endorse what they fail to censor. The ACLJ letter was unapologetic because the rights of Melissa Graham and her friends are substantial. Unless the situation was rectified, we were prepared to file a lawsuit in the appropriate federal court.

After reviewing our letter, the school officials changed their position, and signs went up at Northwest High School proclaiming the message of hope found in Jesus. Another victory was won because students were willing to face the heat in defense of their faith. Melissa and her friends are but one example of the hundreds of files we have opened up on behalf of students from forty-five states.

See You at the Pole

Consider one outcome of the new climate of openness established by the Bridget Mergens case. Small groups of teenagers have created a national movement. In 1989, a group of high school students in the Dallas-Ft. Worth area met around their school flagpole to pray for their campus. In the spring of 1990, Texas Baptist youth leaders were planning a summer conference and wanted to challenge teenagers to pray "in concert" to take the momentum of their conference into the school system. These two ideas came together in one realization. Every campus has a flagpole that provides an easy gathering point. Who knows? Maybe a few thousand will respond . . .

No one could have dreamed what would follow. History was made September 12 at 7:00 A.M. around the flagpole. Forty-eight thousand kids showed up on twelve hundred campuses in four states, far beyond anyone's wildest hopes. The event was the largest prayer function ever held in Texas. Major television and radio news programs covered the story.

By 1991, See You At The Pole (SYATP) had become a national phenomenon and quickly spread abroad, involving 1.5 million in 1993. Reports poured in from Singapore, Canada, the Philippines, Guatemala, Taiwan, Saipan, Russia, Austria, Albania, Romania, and Belgium. Currently, teens are gathering on six continents in twenty-five countries. More than seventy-five ministries help promote the event to children, youth, and adults. The first organized See You At The Pole event established a legacy that continues to build upon the momentum of prayer.

Many of the gatherings reflected bold statements about the meaning of religious freedom. In Red Square in Moscow, eighty youth and adults met near St. Basil's Cathedral. Eleven teens gathered by a statue of a freedom fighter at a formally forbidden park in Targu Mures, Romania. The movement took a new twist in Castro Valley, California. Calling their event "See You At The Stroll," six hundred adults sang and marched two miles to a prayer meeting at a church.

Across America, Christian students developed their own response to the closed-door policy of public schools by gathering outside around the symbol of patriotism and citizenship, the American flag. The early morning fall gatherings for prayer and proclamation became the teens' acts of resistance and witness. Of course, students' constitutionally guaranteed rights of assembly were quickly challenged by school administrators and the ACLU. Recognizing the profound significance of what was becoming a national movement, the American Center stood up for the rights of assemblage in hundreds of situations.

In Michigan, the ACLU tried to block See You At The Pole events across the entire state. Howard Simon, executive director of the Michigan ACLU, sent a letter to state school superintendent Robert Schiller directing him to "take appropriate steps immediately to ensure that school districts not permit any religious activities on school grounds during the school day, either September 15 (SYATP day) or any other day."

Jay warned Schiller that constitutional free speech guarantees would be violated by administrators "if they forbid, censor or inhibit the prayer rally in any manner." Schiller weighed the opinions and told the ACLU he could not oppose SYATP.

Once the American Center defeated them, the ACLU began backpedaling in embarrassment. In a dramatic reversal, Robert Peck, the ACLU's lead spokesman in Washington, D.C., called off the dogs. A potentially tragic situation had become a victory!

In every legal battle over this issue, the American Center prevailed over the ACLU. In the face of opposition from the ACLJ and other Christian legal organizations, many ACLU ideologues are rethinking their own perspective. The civil rights of all Americans, the unborn, pro-life demonstrators, and people of faith, can no longer be discounted in the name of "political correctness."

As a result of these efforts, in 1995 more than *two million students* nationwide took their stand for Christ in front of their schools' flagpoles. Their persistent witness is still reverberating down the halls and corridors of many public places of instruction. We are beginning to see revival in many of our public schools.

Opposition from school officials is now rare and in some instances has been transformed into aid. In Richardson, Texas, fifty students were praying when pranksters showed up with stereos blasting away. A dozen protestors carried signs reading, "We Don't Do Algebra At Your Church. Don't Do Religion In My School." Alan Sumler said, "We're going to try and overpower their prayer with our music this year." Two principals finally intervened to stop the disruption. Carrie Cartwright, one of the intercessors, said, "The protest made me realize we were praying for a purpose." Many of the prayers focused on the protestors. The students knew their witness for Christ was making an eternal difference.

Examples of the new day for Christians in American schools abound. Teachers are apologizing to students for not permitting them to wear clothing with religious messages or read their Bibles in school. Student-led and student-initiated prayers are again occurring at graduation ceremonies and baccalaureate services. School officials are reopening their facilities to religious groups for after-hours use. Christians are no longer on the run.

Hinder Not the Little Children

One never knows where the next battle will be fought. At the ACLJ, we never cease to be amazed at how ridiculous the attacks can be. Take the case of little Shannon Berry for example.

This lovely first grader attended Bayshore Elementary School in Bradenton, Florida. At her young age, Shannon had already developed a vital and exciting faith. During recess, she and a friend were talking about their mutual belief in Jesus. What more encouraging conversation could two children have? Not at Bayshore Elementary School!

A teacher overheard the conversation and immediately told both first graders that "they are not allowed to talk about Jesus at school." ACLJ senior trial counsel Stuart Roth responded to Shannon's mother's request for help and wrote a lengthy demand letter to the attorney representing Bayshore Elementary School. The school officials were reminded that they are ill-equipped and lack any legal warrant to assert absolute control over the thoughts, opinions, and expressions of students.

The Supreme Court has stated:

> In our system, state-operated schools may not be enclaves of totalitarianism. School officials do not possess absolute authority over their students. Students in school as well as out of school are "persons" under our Constitution. They are possessed of

> fundamental rights which the State must respect, just as they themselves must respect their obligations to the State. In our system, students may not be regarded as closed-circuit recipients of only that which the State chooses to communicate. They may not be confined to the expression of those sentiments that are officially approved. In the absence of a specific showing of constitutionally valid reasons to regulate their speech, students are entitled to freedom of expression of their views. As Judge Gewin, speaking for the Fifth Circuit said, officials cannot suppress "expressions of feelings with which they do not wish to contend."[3]

As ludicrous as it sounds, we let the school know first grader Shannon Berry had been made aware that her expressive rights during recess could not substantially interfere with the work of the school or impinge on the rights of other students. However, the issue we made clear to the Bayshore Elementary School system was that the school and its employees must understand that "undifferentiated fear or apprehension of disturbance is not enough to overcome the right of freedom of expression."[4]

The bottom line on senior trial counsel Stuart Roth's letter of support for Shannon was to remind the school, "The Establishment Clause does not license government to treat religion and those who teach or practice it, simply by virtue of their status as such, as subversive of American ideals and therefore subject to unique disabilities."[5] Shannon's religious expression is fully protected under the First Amendment. The censorship of Shannon's speech constitutes content and view-point-based discrimination. Violation of an individual's constitutional rights, even for a moment, results in irreparable injury. We demanded that the school desist and retreat.

Key Issues

In order to carry the battle forward, you need to understand your basic rights and where the lines are drawn. The following are key issues that are protected by the Constitution and recent Supreme Court decisions.

- Bible clubs and religious organizations have the right to advertise on campus. Public address systems, bulletin boards, school newspapers, and normal outlets that are available to other clubs to disseminate their message are open to you.
- *Student-initiated* religious groups are protected. Students may develop groups in order to spread the gospel on campus. Schools must allow students the freedom to start and attend their own meetings on school campuses when the students attend.
- The Supreme Court has made it clear that schools cannot treat Bible clubs or religious organizations differently than other noncurriculum clubs in any way. You have the full right to be treated like any other organization. School officials must give you the same meeting time as other groups and the same ability to get your message out as is provided other students.
- You cannot be prohibited from wearing a shirt with a Christian message or any other message. This right is

protected by the First Amendment. Students cannot be barred from bringing a Bible on campus or into the schoolroom. The student is only bound by an obligation not to disrupt school discipline.

- You have the right to share your faith in your high school. School officials cannot control student speech just because the particular speech is religious in nature. Students have the right to pass out papers, tracts, or any material that expresses their viewpoint to their peers. In the *Mergens* case, the Court's opinion made it clear that a student's right to share his or her faith does not interfere with other students' rights.
- Your rights extend to the classroom, the cafeteria, and the playing field outside. You can surround the flagpole. No one can keep you from praying silently wherever you choose. However, when students gather as a group during their free time, they are guaranteed such basic rights, including corporate prayer.

The Next Step

Now the battle begins! You have the right to assemble, but you have to use it. God has opened up a tremendous mission field in the American school system. The responsibility is now ours. We have to go through the door the Supreme Court has opened to us. The matter is in your hands today.

See You At The Pole is a powerful example of what happens when the opportunity is seized. Following the 1995 rally, a web page was opened on the Internet. A multitude of "cyber-testimonies" followed. One student e-mailed in, "Because of

SYATP, I recently started a Bible study with one of my teachers. In just 3 weeks, we already have 15 people (I go to a rather small school). The Lord is really at work!" Another typed in, "I go to a public school in Knoxville, TN and nothing feels as good as unifying with other Christians in prayer for the year ahead. Every year our circle gets bigger and bigger—maybe this year we'll cover the parking lot!" Identified only as Laura W78, the student reported, "This is my fourth year doing SYATP. Each year it has been a great time of prayer for my school, and last year we had 6 kids come out. This year we had 32 students and 2 teachers pray at SYATP! Praise God!" These students used the moment God gave them to bring glory to His name.

The ACLJ is committed to bringing every school board in America into compliance with the legal rights guaranteed to all Christians. If you encounter obstinate school officials and discriminatory rules, contact us, and we will stand with you. Someday we must all give account of our lives before the Great Throne of God. Can you think of a better defense than to know you were on the offensive for the Kingdom of God in these times of transition?

CHAPTER 7

TO PRAY OR NOT TO PRAY

THE ISSUE in our schools is much deeper than legal rights. The battle is also between competing faiths. The new religion has already begun to move into place! In fact, the opposition is already firmly entrenched in the school system. Christians must continue to stand up for the gospel.

The Simpsons Go to Church

The First "Church" of Secularism is doing its job quite well. Without steeple or cross, this new system of belief doesn't require its adherents to show up for any services on the weekend. To the contrary, the secularists send their people to the mountains or the lakes with the admonition, "Don't waste time thinking about God." The secularist "church" endorses pleasure and promotes self-indulgence.

Pulpits are too old fashioned for free-thinking secular humanists, but they are big on magazines and publications. *Humanist* magazine has the message of the moment. You only get the "moment," as nothing is absolute or enduring in this church! Here's a sample of a missionary message.

> I am convinced that the battle for humankind's future must be waged and won in the public school classroom by teachers who correctly perceive their role as the proselytizers of the new faith: a religion of humanity. . . . These teachers must embody the same selfless dedication as the most rabid fundamentalist preachers, for they will be ministers of another sort, utilizing a classroom instead of a pulpit to convey humanist values in whatever they teach. . . . The classroom must and will become an arena of conflict between the old and the new—the rotting corpse of Christianity.[1]

You can bet Bart Simpson and his family are wild about this alternative religion. You may be surprised to know secular humanism is now perceived as the nation's civil religion. *That's one reason why there is so much flak over prayer in the public schools!*

Of course, there is no First Church of Secularism listed in the yellow pages or to be found on America's Main Street. The religion doesn't have pews and stained glass, but it certainly has its preachers and teachers. Secular humanism is a philosophy with the goal of replacing Christian morals with a nondemanding relativism that is anti-God!

Following the 1962 Supreme Court decision that struck down state-sponsored prayer in the public schools, secular humanists were on a roll. The continuing attack on prayer in the public arena is simply one dimension of the ongoing pressure to demolish the Christian presence.

The Faith Under Siege

The evidence of assault is strewn across the historical landscape of the last thirty years. The attack has taken many strange and disheartening turns. A Chicago school teacher ended up in a lawsuit because she led her kindergarten students in a simple prayer before enjoying milk and cookies. In 1962, the Sixth Circuit Court of Appeals stopped the practice, forbidding students even to fold their hands and close their eyes, obvious subversive actions.

In Albany, New York, Students for Voluntary Prayer sought official recognition from their high school in order to use an empty classroom to meet before school for prayer. The principal turned their request down. When the students protested and sued, the principal's decision was upheld in a federal district court and the Second Circuit Court of Appeals. The court said permitting the meeting would have violated the First Amendment Establishment clause prohibiting the state from establishing religion. The Court of Appeals was sufficiently alarmed to note that even a hint of school approval for the students was "too dangerous to permit."

Stunned Christians across America watched incredulously

as prayer in school became as subversive as profanity on television once was. One step led to another, and soon any practice that reflected prayer or practiced intercession was under suspicion. Confusion proliferated in every village, town, and city in the land.

But faithful people have demonstrated that prayer can't be silenced.

Rocky Mountain Low

At the edge of the Rocky Mountains is the community of Lafayette, virtually a suburb of Boulder, Colorado. Pastor James Ryles came to the community in 1981 and developed a strong, significant Vineyard Fellowship. Former Colorado University coach Bill McCartney is a member of the church, and Ryles is well known for his work with McCartney's Promise Keepers. The four Ryles children are equally well known for their Christian witness in the local schools. Each one has left an outstanding mark on the school.

James Ryles took each of his kids through a rite of passage when they became thirteen. He believed the Hebrew model of a bar mitzvah ceremony validating manhood would help accelerate sons David and Jonathan into greater spiritual maturity. This spiritual maturity equipped both brothers for the battle on their school campus.

As a junior, David made a run for Head Boy, the student body president. His objective was not the office but the opportunity to make a speech to the entire student assembly. For an entire year, he campaigned to prepare for one golden moment. When the day came, David was ready.

Confident that the Holy Spirit would give him the right words, David began his address in a most unusual manner. He said, "In 1972, abortion was legal. Since that day and now millions have died. Today we must remember those aborted babies because they are our classmates. They would have been our boyfriends, girlfriends, our colleagues, and possible leadership, but they are not here today. We are here, but it may be we don't have the right people from which to choose."

The huge assembly became intensely quiet. Students stared in silence. David knew as soon as he finished his next few sentences, he would be forced to stop. He took a deep breath and forged ahead. "But I've found a leader we can trust. There are no posters with His picture on our walls but I know Him personally, and you can too. In fact, I've given my life to Him and He's given His life to us. That person is Jesus Christ."

Before David could say anything more, the principal leaped up and grabbed the microphone. "You're done," he snapped and took the microphone away. Even though the school administrator clearly broke the law violating David's constitutional right of free speech, David had made a decisive stand for Christ.

For the next two weeks, a storm raged through the school. Many applauded, many were appalled, but few were neutral. David had done a manly thing and didn't back off. During the next year, teachers recognized the significance of David's conviction and often would say, "David, tell the class a story out of the 'book' you carry." David would relate a Bible story. The ripples from his Head Boy speech continued on month after month.

The legacy of David's stand gave eleventh-grader Jonathan,

the last of the Ryles brood, the courage and confidence to form a group for prayer and Bible study in Centaurus High School. John, a large, athletic-looking young man with brown eyes and a bleached-blond flat-top haircut, wasn't interested in making points or being difficult. He was simply a young man who loved God and wanted the right to express that devotion in the place where he spent most of his time—his school.

He first approached the assistant principal with his proposal to form the group and then was sent on to the principal. He knew his brother's reputation would be somewhat involved in how he was treated. John noted that nearby St. Vrain School district allowed these activities. John wasn't surprised when his request for the establishment of an on-campus Christian group was turned down.

Principal William Johnson refused John's request on the grounds it "would not be allowed because it would violate the Constitution." When John's request was rebuffed, he turned to the ACLJ for help, and deputy chief counsel Joel Thornton handled the case. The ACLJ sent a demand letter to the school.

The ensuing discussion with the officials revealed a new dimension to the battle over religion in schools. Centaurus High School practiced a closed-campus policy, which did not allow any noncurricular groups access to the school system. Because of a closed campus, the school could legally refuse to assign a room to John's group. John's club could not use the usual means of advertising and communication or be included in the school yearbook. The way was opened, however, for John's group to meet as a student-initiated activity. No one could stop John and his friends from gathering spontaneously and praying right where they were.

John was asked what he learned from pursuing the issue. He said, "I discovered that it is possible to change things. I didn't get all that I wanted, but the future is open. People at the top know about my request. Tomorrow may be different." John was not silenced by the school's closed-campus policy.

Key School Prayer Cases

What is the legal situation students and teachers face when they want to pray in school? Because of close scrutiny by the Supreme Court, many well-intentioned school officials have been fearful of running afoul of the law. Administrators need to know that the central issue of the problem has always been around school-mandated, required, or composed prayers.

In *Engle v. Vitale,* the original issue was the constitutionality of a daily ritual mandated by the state of New York. Public school classes were required at the direction of the school officials to recite a prayer written by the authorities. At the beginning of each school day, immediately after the Pledge of Allegiance, a teacher or selected student led the class in saying, "Almighty God, we acknowledge our dependence upon Thee, and we beg Thy blessings upon us, our parents, our teachers, and our country."

The Supreme Court's response was negative. The justices instructed, "It is no part of the business of government to compose official prayers for any group of the American people to recite as a part of a religious program carried on by the government."[2]

The *Abington v. Schempp* ruling was similar. In this instance, the state *required* the reading of the Holy Bible and the recitation of the Lord's Prayer at the start of the day. The pressing issue was that these religious exercises were on school property with direct oversight of government-employed teachers. In addition, the practices were prescribed as part of the curricular activities of students required by law to attend school.[3]

Significantly, the Court qualified its position in the *Schempp* opinion, stating a positive view of religious discussion: "It certainly may be said that the Bible is worthy of study for its literary and historic qualities. Nothing we have said here indicates that such study of the Bible or religion, when presented objectively as part of a secular program of education, may not be effected consistently with the First Amendment."[4]

As a result of these early opinions, however, many school officials overreacted and became hostile toward all private expressions of religious views in the public schools. They missed the seminal issue, the forbidden role of government in enforcing its own chosen forms of religious expression. The result was the censorship of private speech of students expressing personal religious ideals. David Ryle's speech to the student body was protected by this fact. The principal missed the principle.

They Can't "Tinker" with You!

The Supreme Court clearly addressed the rights of students to express themselves in public schools in a case named, interestingly enough, *Tinker v. Des Moines Independent Community School District.* The suit involved students who wore black armbands to protest the Vietnam war. School officials tried to halt such expressions. The sharp response of the Supreme Court has proved to be good news for Christians: "It can hardly be argued that either students or teachers can shed their constitutional rights to freedom of speech or expression at the schoolhouse gate. This has been the unmistakable holding of this Court for almost 50 years."[5] The only inhibition to student speech is some form of interference with the discipline involved in the operation of the school. The Court was clear that school officials do not possess absolute authority over students. "Students in school as well as out of school are 'persons' under our Constitution."[6]

Nevertheless, lots of "tinkering" has gone on in the American school systems. Hostile administrators errantly mandated prohibitions of *all* prayers at graduations and forbade students to discuss religious views in valedictory or salutatory speeches.

What Are Your Rights?

What if you chose to make such a difference? You would need to know how these legal decisions impact your right to pray at school. The following are answers to frequently asked questions on this subject.

Q. *Can students lead prayer at graduation ceremonies?*

A. *Yes. The critical difference between schools endorsing religion and the rights of private citizens to free speech endorsing religion or prayer is central to what the Free Speech and Free Exercise Clauses uphold. In* Lee v. Weisman, *the Supreme Court held only that it violates the Establishment Clause for school officials to invite clergy to give prayers at commencement. Justice Kennedy made clear, for the majority, that the Court's decision was limited to the particular facts before the Court. Thus, any change from the*

factual situation presented in Lee might alter the resulting opinion from the Court.

Indeed, following Lee, at least one Federal Appeals Court has ruled that "a majority of students can do what the State acting on its own cannot do to incorporate prayer in public high school graduation ceremonies." In *Jones v. Clear Creek Independent School District (Jones II),* a post-Lee decision, the Fifth Circuit upheld the constitutionality of a school district resolution permitting high school seniors to include a student-led invocation in their graduation ceremony if the majority of the class so votes. Quite unlike the school-directed and school-controlled practice found unconstitutional in Lee, the Clear Creek Independence School District's resolution simply permits the students of each graduating class to decide if they do or do not wish to have an invocation as a part of their commencement. In the event that students choose to include an invocation, the resolution provides that it shall be nonsectarian and nonproselytizing and conducted only by a student volunteer.

The Jones II Court recognized, as the Supreme Court has previously held, that "there is a crucial difference between government speech endorsing religion, which the Establishment Clause forbids, and private speech endorsing religion, which the Free Speech and Free Exercise Clauses protect.

The Fifth Circuit is the only United States Court of Appeals to have addressed the rights of students to initiate prayers at graduation following the Supreme Court's decision in *Lee v. Weisman.* On June 7, 1993, the Supreme Court denied certiorari in Jones II. In other words, the Supreme Court let stand the Fifth Circuit Court of Appeals's decision permitting student-initiated prayer at graduation. Thus, the Fifth Circuit's opinion in Jones II provides school boards across the nation, both within and outside the Fifth Circuit, with a valid legal basis for choosing to uphold the rights of students to initiate prayers at graduation.

Some may suggest that the school officials should aggressively censor all student expression simply because it occurs within the jurisdiction of the school. The law regarding the First Amendment rights of students is well-established, however. Student speech cannot be restricted because of the content of that speech.

Q. ***Do students have the right to pray together at school?***

A. ***Yes. Students always retain their constitutional rights of free speech and expression, which include the right to pray and share personal beliefs. See You At The Pole National Day of Prayer is a student-led and student-initiated event. On an annual basis, students across the nation gather with like-minded peers around the flagpole at their respective schools before the class day begins and pray for their schools, teachers, administrators, and country.***

As we discussed earlier in this book, students retain their constitutional rights of free speech and expression, including the right to pray and share personal beliefs, while on their public school campuses. Under the Tinker standard, school officials may restrict protected student speech only if it "materially and substantially interfere[s] with appropriate discipline." Thus, school officials may not prevent students from gathering together for prayer and religious discussion on school grounds, provided that students do so in a noninstructional time. Noninstructional time would be immediately before and after school, at lunchtime, or any other "free" time when students are permitted to talk and mingle with peers on campus.

It should be noted that while school officials may not prevent students from engaging in protected religious expression unless it "materially and substantially interferes with school discipline," they may impose reasonable time, place, and manner restrictions. Such restrictions, however, must be content-neutral, "narrowly tailored to serve a significant government interest, and leave open ample alternative channels of communication."

Q. ***Are official "moments of silence" permitted?***

A. ***Yes! The Supreme Court reviewed the issue of official "moments of silence" in*** **Wallace v. Jaffree.** ***While it is true that the Supreme Court did find the particular "moment of silence" statute before the Court in that case unconstitutional, the Wallace Court did not declare that all "moments of silence" violate the Establishment Clause. In fact, a majority of the Wallace Court clearly recognized that moments of silence are constitutionally permissible: "I agree fully with Justice O'Connor's assertion that some moment-of-silence statutes may be constitutional, a suggestion set forth in the Court's opinion as well." Furthermore, all parties in the Wallace case agreed that an Alabama statute mandating a "moment of silence" during classtime was constitutional. Wallace held only that the particular facts of the case made the Alabama statute calling for a moment of silence "for meditation or voluntary prayer" during classtime unconstitutional. Specifically, the Court focused on the clearly religious intent expressed by the statute's sponsors in the***

recorded legislative history, and the express language of the statute, which called for a moment of silence "for meditation or voluntary prayer."

After Wallace, it is clear that any official moment of silence must be motivated by a well-defined secular purpose and be neutral on its face, leaving the use of the "moment of silence" to individuals and the dictates of their own consciences.

Q. ***Can students have baccalaureate services?***

A. ***Yes. Students, community groups, and area churches are entitled to sponsor events such as baccalaureate services. If school facilities are available to the community for use, these groups must be allowed to use school facilities also, regardless of the religious nature of their activities. A policy of equal access for religious speech conveys a message "of neutrality rather than endorsement; if a State refused to let religious groups use facilities open to others, then it would demonstrate not neutrality but hostility toward religion." The United States District Court for the District of Wyoming recently issued a preliminary injunction allowing a baccalaureate service in a public high school. The court relied directly on Lamb's Chapel.***

Q. ***Can a prayer meeting be held even if it is not part of an officially recognized club on campus?***

A. ***Yes. Prayer is a protected form of speech that cannot be banned by school officials. School officials refusal of students' right to pray on campus is nothing short of censorship. Such events as See You At The Pole are covered.***

Q. ***Can Christmas still be identified as a Christmas vacation?***

A ***Yes. Constitutional requirements do not exist for re-***

naming holidays such as Christmas vacation as "winter vacation." The Supreme Court acknowledged the ability of Congress to give federal employees a paid Christmas holiday on December 25.

Students have the right to express their beliefs and convictions as they apply to holidays like Hanukkah, Christmas, and Easter. Thanksgiving pictures may be drawn with pictures of pilgrims praying to God. When given the right to choose a topic, a student may write about the birth of Christ or any other religious topic. They have the right to express their feelings about the value of prayer.

Let's Get the Word Out

The president of the United States has specially directed that the secretary of education inform school districts regarding religious expression in public schools. In a July 12, 1995, memorandum to the secretary and to the attorney general, President Bill Clinton affirmed the principles we have presented. Calling religious freedom "perhaps the most precious of all American liberties," he pointed out that "our nation's founders knew that religion helps to give our people the character without which a democracy cannot survive."

Commenting on the unfortunate incidents like the ones David and Jonathan Ryles faced, the president noted: "It appears that some school officials, teachers, and parents have assumed that religious expression of any type is either inappropriate or forbidden altogether in public schools; however, nothing in the First Amendment converts our public schools into religion-free zones. . . . the government's schools . . . may not discriminate against private religious expression during the school day." Further, he noted that while school officials "have substantial discretion to impose rules of order, they may not structure or administer such rules to discriminate against religious activity or speech."[7]

Multitudes have prayed for these changes, and obviously prayer worked! Let's take the president at his word, take the message out, and keep on praying.

CHAPTER 8

THE ABORTION DISTORTION

RESPECTFUL QUIET fell across the immense gathering of national leaders as the small speaker made her way to the microphone. The National Prayer Breakfast assembled the Congress and all other branches of government with the president of the United States on February 3, 1994, to pause and intercede for the country. Prominent religious leaders traveled to Washington, D.C., annually to join the prayer meeting and hear an internationally known spiritual authority.

The political dignitaries on the center platform towered

over the little eighty-three-year-old nun as the crowd welcomed her. As Mother Teresa spoke of caring for the vulnerable and the unwanted, her natural dignity and grace gave her remarks an aura of profound spirituality. The assembly of the powerful strained forward to catch every word. Although the breakfast represented the ultimate gathering of world might, petite Mother Teresa was clearly a symbol of yet a greater power.

The nun received loud applause throughout her speech and lavish praise afterward. Her statements were immediately dispatched nationally and internationally. And yet at the climax of her speech, as the dignitaries stood, the president, vice president, and their wives sat stone-faced. Mother Teresa said in accented but perfect English:

> I feel that the greatest destroyer of peace today is abortion, because it is war against the child, a direct killing of the innocent child, murder by the mother herself. . . .
> By abortion, the mother does not learn to love, but kills even her own child to solve her problems. And by abortion, the father is told that he does not have to take any responsibility at all for the child he has brought into the world. That father is likely to put other women into the same trouble. So abortion just leads to more abortion. Any country that accepts abortion is not teaching its people to love, but to use violence to get what they want. This is why the greatest destroyer of love and peace is abortion.

The simplicity of this genuinely humble woman pointed out the truth of a current pattern of terror masquerading in the halls of Congress as the public policy of the United States of America.

The Nakedness of the Emperor

Remember the old children's story of the emperor's search for the finest fabric and the greatest tailor to weave an inaugural gown worthy of his ascension to the throne of his country? The clever tailor convinced the king that the tailor's cloth was so fine it could not even be seen by the human eye. As the day of coronation approached, the monarch was convinced he was robed in the finest garments ever made. The gathered crowd cheered when he appeared on the balcony to begin the festivities.

Only a child had the lucidity to tell the truth. "Look!" he shouted. "The emperor is naked!" Applause turned to laughter as the emperor's foolish pretentiousness was unmasked. Mother Teresa's honest, straightforward message showed government claims of compassion to be equally pretentious . . . and empty.

The transparent delusion is that the nation gives lip service to concern for the vulnerable, needy, and poor while enacting government programs enabling abortion. We continue to call the killing of our progeny "reproductive rights." The shameful truth is that abortion is neither reproductive nor right!

A little nun from India, who has spent her life holding close the dying and poverty stricken because she still sees their inherent dignity and value, revealed that rich America has no clothes. She finished her speech by calling us to a better course: "If we remember that God loves us and that we can love others as He loves us, then America can become a sign of peace for the world. From here, a sign of care for the weakest of the weak—the unborn child—must go out to the world." The ACLJ accepts Mother Teresa's challenge to go forth and make the world safe for the yet-to-be-born.

Standing with the Accused

"I cannot in good conscience pay that fine," Operation Rescue leader Randall Terry said respectfully as he turned down a deal from Fulton County judge John Brunner. Jay stood at Randall's side, as he would on other occasions, supporting the pro-life advocate. Randall Terry was trying to fulfill Mother Teresa's challenge. He had been offered a suspended two-year prison sentence if he would pay a $500 fine and stay out of Atlanta for two years. He could not.

While Randall was technically representing himself in court, Jay was coaching him on how to proceed. He was charged with unlawful assembly and trespassing at an abortion clinic as part of a mass protest rally during the Democratic National Convention. The two acts of civil disobedience were minor, but the court's overreaction was major.

Jay knew Randall had been found not guilty on similar charges in Los Angeles. In addition, in a unanimous opinion involving participants in the same Atlanta rescue incident, the Georgia Court of Appeals held that the people blocking the doors to the clinic could not be found guilty of both trespassing and unlawful assembly at the same time. But when the judge was asked to apply that decision, he refused. Jay pleaded the case until the bailiff asked him to sit down. In this travesty of justice, the judge did not even allow Randall to present his case to the jury. Randall Terry was later released from jail after serving four and a half months of his two-year sentence because someone anonymously paid the fine.

In February 1992, five students at the University of Virginia were arrested for blocking an entrance to an off-campus abortion clinic. Subsequently, a fellow student accused them of violating a student judicial code. The five were brought before the student judiciary committee. A student leader admitted to one of our attorneys that the charges were brought because the protestors' actions were not "politically correct." The ACLJ was able to demonstrate that the protestors were protected by the First Amendment, and the harassment stopped.

In January 1991, the Department of Women's Services at Ohio State University refused to allow a student pro-life organization inclusion in its annual information brochure. Department directors claimed the group oppressed women by denying them their full range of reproductive choices. Because the pro-life viewpoint did not agree with the department's political agenda, the First Amendment rights of students were grossly violated.

In the name of equal opportunity, the "politically correct" authorities advocate atheism, feminism, and homosexuality while denying the free exercise of Christianity. Our experience in the Ohio case demonstrated that the pride American universities take in "open-mindedness" is, in a great many instances, a myth. The PC agenda is specific, well defined, and diametrically opposed to Christianity and to First Amendment freedoms.

Randall Terry and the hundreds following him have a keen

sense of the gross injustice of abortion, and they are willing to pay the price. We have felt the same burden when standing in court with those who feel that they must obey God's laws when they are in conflict with humanity's misguided attempts at social legislation.

The Sixth Commandment

The Bible prohibits murder, and this is the primary issue in the morality of abortion. God hasn't removed "Thou shalt not kill" from the Top Ten. The abortionists want the public to believe life begins at birth so that their procedures aren't considered killing. The biblical view is much broader and more profound.

Jeremiah 1:5 states, "Then the word of the LORD came to me, saying: 'Before I formed you in the womb I knew you; before you were born I sanctified you." The psalmist said, "For Thou didst form my inward parts; Thou didst weave me in my mother's womb. I will give thanks to Thee, for I am fearfully and wonderfully made; wonderful are Thy works, And my soul knows it very well." Similarly the first chapter of Luke tells the story of the unborn son of Elizabeth, John the Baptist, leaping in his mother's womb at Mary's greeting. The Bible clearly extends the beginning of life back to the moment of conception.

Today we know that an eighteen-week-old fetus has a nose, lips, hands, fingers, and ears. At that point the unborn can move and respond to touch. This fetus will not be fully developed until around twenty-one years of age. Nevertheless, current law allows more than four thousand of these yet-to-be-born children to be killed every day in this country.

In the 1973 Supreme Court's *Roe v. Wade* abortion decision, the rights of the unborn were put in a similar category with the rights of blacks in the last century. The infamous Dred Scott decision of 1857 denied the essential rights of blacks with the consequence that killing a person of color could not be grounds for homicide in a court of law. As frightening as that remnant of history is, we are still locked into the same mentality when it comes to the rights of the unborn.

The ACLJ will not allow this situation to go unchallenged.

The Holocaust of the "Least of These"

No battle has resulted in the pain and taken the toll of human life as has the carnage of legalized abortion. Prior to the *Roe v. Wade* decision, the official estimates of abortions performed yearly went from a low of 39,000 in 1950 to a high of 210,000 in 1961 with a mean annual abortion rate of 98,000.[1] After the legalization of abortion in 1973, the annual rate soared to 744,600 a year and soon reached 1.6 million.[2] Currently, one out of every three babies conceived in America is aborted! In more than fourteen metropolitan areas, abortions outnumber live births. Abortion claims the lives of 131,520 children every month, 4,384 each day, 183 each hour, 3 each minute, and 1 every twenty seconds.[3] Through abortion alone, America has killed about four times more people than the combined number of adults, adolescents, and children who lost their lives under the extermination policies of Nazi Germany. Eclipsing the Third Reich, America has gone after her most vulnerable with a vengeance.

In past civilized societies, abortion was openly labeled

murder. America now calls it "a woman's choice," "reproductive rights," "birth control," "menstrual extraction," "planned parenting," or "a life-rationing procedure." Regardless of the verbal engineering, abortion is still the intentional killing of a human being. It's still murder.

If anyone ever needed an attorney, it is these tiny, helpless human beings who have no voice in their own destinies. Their right to life was not stripped because they committed some crime or were at war with anyone. They were simply terminated by more powerful people. The ACLJ is doing everything possible to stand with the defenseless.

The Termination Generation

We want you to meet another person profoundly affected by the new permissive climate. In her picture, this beautiful, petite two-year-old girl is posing in a white-lace dress, matching leotards, and buckled white dress shoes. For the sake of anonymity, let's call our little friend Mary. Her big brown eyes and curly dark hair could melt the coldest heart. Mary is perfect in every way except for one problem. This child is missing an arm.

Here is the rest of the story. The child's problem is the result of a botched abortion. In an attempt to terminate the pregnancy at eight months, her arm was torn off. A physician in New York failed to complete his deadly task. The story came to light because the abortionist was prosecuted, not for trying to save the girl's life but for failing to carry out effectively her death sentence.[4]

The same week the child's story appeared, an interview

with the feminist president of the local chapter of the National Organization for Women (NOW) was published. The leader decried efforts to make abortion less available. Bristling at the thought of pro-life demonstrators, she told the reporter, "At any other business or place you couldn't have this kind of behavior trying to keep customers or clients out." She gestured to a waitress to refill her Coca-Cola.[5] Abortion was nothing more than a business, a consumer issue just like ordering a soft drink in a restaurant.

In 1973 the U.S. Supreme Court in one collective stroke of the pen changed the terms of the defense of human life. Conveniently discerning the "penumbra" (shadow) of the Constitution ensuring a right to privacy, the justices shoehorned the nation into the abortion distortion. Consequently, the courtroom has become a combat zone.

But the real shadow fell over millions of the unborn. Their existence became the target for assault. The Court decided against the unborn by ignoring an explicit statement of their rights found in the Declaration of Independence. "We hold these truths to be self-evident, that all men are created equal, that they are endowed by their Creator with certain unalienable rights, that among these are *life,* liberty and the pursuit of happiness." The founders of this country saw clearly that creation is a divine act, not just a sex act. They knew *all* human life has *an unalienable right* to exist. The 1972 decision flew in the face of these truths.

Mary's missing arm and the silent multitude of her lost playmates are the results of the deadly penumbra.

In the same arbitrary manner, the Court contrived its own definition of when life begins. The normal flow of human fetal development was broken up into trimesters. In the first three months of life, abortion was without restriction. During the next three months, states can regulate but not deny abortion. In the last period, states can stop abortion if the mother's physical or mental health is not endangered. However, these restrictions are so vague, the resultant "abortion on demand" permeates the country. Most of the states' attempts to modify the situation have been found to be unconstitutional. Obviously, the ACLJ has its work cut out in trying to protect the "termination generation."

Who Is the Enemy?

When the Nazis came for the Jews in the Warsaw ghetto, the oppressors were easy to identify. Swastikas and military uniforms were obvious. At the Auschwitz death camp, the commandant wore black leather boots and an army cap. But how shall we identify the enemy snuffing out a life every twenty seconds?

John Courtney Murray, the great Jesuit theologian and teacher, has already warned us not to be deceived by the genteel look of the new oppressors.

> The barbarian need not appear in bearskins with a club in hand. He may wear a Brooks Brothers suit and carry a ballpoint pen with which to write his advertising copy. In fact, even beneath the academic gown there may lurk a child of the wilderness, untutored in the high tradition of civility, who goes busily and happily about his work, a domesticated and law-abiding man, engaged in the construction of a philosophy to put an end to all philosophy, and thus put to

an end the possibility of a vital consensus and to civility itself.[6]

John Courtney Murray believed the American experiment was a historical one of the highest expressions of the idea of social consensus. Murray understood that such a development is a hallmark of civilization. If the new secularists in Gucci shoes are able to destroy the nation's sense of goodness and distort our view of social evil, they will undermine the very foundations that hold Americans together as one people. The voices trying to tell us death is life and convince us that destruction is creative are destroying the common social fabric that has made us one nation under God.

Murray said further: "This is perennially the work of the barbarian, to undermine rational standards of judgment, to corrupt the inherited intuitive wisdom by which people have always lived, and to do this not by spreading new beliefs but by creating a climate of doubt and bewilderment in which clarity about the larger aims of life is dimmed and the self-confidence of the people is destroyed, so that finally what you have is an impotent nihilism."[7]

Father Murray warned of the approaching peril more than thirty-five years ago, well before the Court's terrible decision. Today the social engineers continue to push us toward the substitution of a culture of death for what has been a society of life. The ACLJ is determined to do everything humanly possible to stand against this assault from the cultured enemies of life. No one can convince us that it is moral to do the immoral.

One of the ultimate ironies in the contemporary history of

government-sponsored death comes to us now from—of all places—Germany! The German Supreme Court recently ruled that unborn children have a constitutionally protected right to life, beginning at conception. The only woman justice on the Court rightly ruled in favor of life.[8] Could the nation that once embraced the ethic of death as national policy lead us back to national sanity?

More than twenty years after Justice Harry A. Blackmun put his pen to the *Roe v. Wade* decision, he issued a dissenting opinion in a case involving the death penalty. "From this day forward, I no longer shall tinker with the machinery of death. I feel morally and intellectually obligated simply to concede that the death penalty experiment has failed."[9] And yet with a simple signature the justice had participated in setting the machinery of death in motion whereby unborn human beings can be dismembered, burned by saline solution, or sucked out of the womb. The duplicity of the justice's decision is now painfully obvious.

Meet the New Advocates for Life

The ACLJ has assembled staff to fight on every possible front in the war against abortion. One of our key lawyers is Thomas Patrick Monaghan.

"Pat" Monaghan and Professor Charles Rice of the University of Notre Dame School of Law were co-founders of Free Speech Advocates, a project of Catholics United for Life. Like the popular country song, "I Was Country When Country Wasn't Cool," Pat Monaghan was pro-life when the position wasn't in. He was in a pro-life law practice when representation meant maxing out his credit card to participate in the new civil rights movement.

A devout conservative Roman Catholic Christian, Pat is a gifted and dedicated warrior in our alliance of evangelical Protestants, Jewish believers in Jesus, Roman Catholics, and Orthodox. Notre Dame professor Charles Rice has joined us as a senior fellow of the ACLJ. As one of the foremost constitutional scholars in the country, he is also a prolific author and tireless advocate, bringing to us an intellectual wellspring of scholarship, insight, and experience.

You Can Make a Difference

Like many grief-stricken Americans, you may feel helpless and impotent in this current quagmire of moral contradictions. Unfortunately, some despairing protestors have been pushed into acts of violence, only making the problem worse. Other Christians have sunk into disillusioned resignation, doing nothing. Neither alternative is biblically sound. You *can* make a difference even in this dark hour. Here are concrete steps.

Know the Facts

Many Americans are startled to discover that millions of lives have been sacrificed through abortion. Obviously, this country has been practicing birth control by death for a long time. The simple fact that a life is terminated every twenty seconds gives thoughtful people pause. Even right-of-choice supporters blink when they discover we have far surpassed anything the Nazis accomplished in exterminating human beings.

You can help people understand the issue isn't political correctness but moral rightness. Society doesn't allow "pro-choice" in killing parents with Alzheimer's disease or terminating the lives of the profoundly retarded. Courts are clear that people aren't left to make up their minds whether or not they agree with laws forbidding theft, burglary, and assault. Even in a democracy, we don't have a choice when it comes to damaging other lives.

Get the message out to your friends!

Understand the Issues

Public opinion is molded and shaped by advocates of the truth who tell their story in straightforward forceful terms. You need to be informed about the errors in the *Roe v. Wade* decision.

First, let people know that the original defendant in this case, Norma Jean McCorvey, has now repented of and recanted her actions. After she worked in an abortion clinic for a short while and then became an evangelical Christian, the meaning of abortion overwhelmed McCorvey. Pro-choice advocates are embarrassed that the "Jane Roe" in the initial case has repudiated her actions. The woman's desire to reverse her decision speaks volumes.

Pat Monaghan has helped all of us understand more profoundly the abiding unconstitutionality and illegitimacy of *Roe v. Wade.* Acquaint yourself with his insights into the issues. Share the larger truth with others. Monaghan has written: "Clearly, the deliberate authorization by court or legislature of the execution of innocent human beings (who, of course, are persons) is in violation of the Fifth and Fourteenth Amendments of the United States Constitution as well as the moral vision of the Declaration of Independence, the *fons et origo* of our constitutional republic."[10]

The Fifth and Fourteenth Amendments stand as our guarantee of protection and right to inclusion in the national family. These amendments ensure no person shall be deprived of "life, liberty or property without due process of law."

The present blindness of the Supreme Court is only another indication of the current barbarism called modernity. At issue is our traditional national ethic granting intrinsic worth to all humanity, regardless of stage in life or condition of health.

Pat Monaghan has described our current madness in clear terms:

> When the word "person" is manipulated to deny the right to life to human flesh and blood, but the same word is used to grant rights and privileges to an inanimate corporation, the semantic gymnastics cease being "curious" and "ludicrous" and become grotesque. "Person" as a legalism can be expanded to include General Motors. But at the least, in realism, it must include all human beings. Otherwise, the word "person" in the Fifth and Fourteenth Amendments is meaningless to humans as offering them any protection. In the *Abortion Cases,* "person" has become a metaphor without reference. It is like saying Paul Newman is a star, but Alpha Centauri is not, or that the members of the Supreme Court embody justice, but God does not.[11]

You can insist that abortion is not about the disposal of tissue but the death of persons.

Don't Give Up on Legislative Efforts.

Legislators remain sensitive to these issues. NOW and Planned Parenthood have a large war chest but no moral persuasion. In 1994, 260 percent more pro-life legislation was proposed in state houses than was proposed in 1993. The year 1995 witnessed even more pro-life legislation than in the previous year. Many comrades are still fighting the battle in government.

Communities *can* change. In fact, Chattanooga, Tennessee, is an excellent example of a peaceful metamorphosis accomplished by Christians who kept working the political processes. By carefully organizing the breadth of the Christian community into a unified force, the leaders pursued only avenues of nonviolent peaceful expression. They marshaled many volunteers into the cause. In 1992, 1,086 abortions were performed in this community, but by 1993 only 463 abortions were performed. By 1994 the rate was reduced to 39. Now there are no abortion clinics in the community. Pro-life leaders bought the last abortion mill, not only putting the clinic out of business but also turning the place into a memorial to the lost children.

No one knows when a new perspective, angle, or insight may surface and result in a political breakthrough. This is not a time for retreat but for reengagement with the enemy.

Pray!

Remember when we thought prayer and the Bible had been permanently ripped out of the classroom? During discouraging times faithful people continued to pray. America's unseen intercessors may yet be revealed as the most powerful external force at work in our society. No one can calculate exactly what prayer accomplishes, but with prayer, we can easier recognize the result when the hand of God moves.

Ask your church to pray for us in worship services. Request your prayer groups to intercede without ceasing. When you become tired, remember the example of the little prayer warrior nun from Calcutta whom God used to witness to the most powerful political leaders in this country. Our God does still reign!

CHAPTER 9

WHEN DEATH WALKS THE STREET

ACEDIA IS no longer a terribly common word, but it should be. Often the word is considered a synonym for sloth, for laziness, but neither is quite accurate and comprehensive enough. The meaning of this word must be recovered if we are to understand why our country is caught in the current moral upheaval resulting in a prevailing atmosphere of death.

The word helps us understand why television programs are saturated with stories of murder, rape, violence, and mayhem. The term clarifies why movies are filled with gratuitous sex and unsatisfying relationships—and why the ACLJ's fight for life extends beyond the abortion struggle.

Let's paint a word picture of acedia.

A high school student wears a T-shirt to school stamped on the front with a bloody skull with monster eyes. On the back are the words "No Fear!" His bedroom is covered with posters of grotesque creatures with bulging superhero muscles, smashing through walls and knocking people's heads off. The student has a large picture over his desk of a shirtless heavy metal rock musician belting out obscene lyrics to a song about the glories of homosexuality. The youth's parents are terrified that he may become a victim of one of the weekly drive-by shootings in their community. They have already been to two funerals for peers who were victims of gang violence.

The school's dress code will only allow the teenager to go so far. Nevertheless, he does everything possible to cultivate a degenerate look. Baggy pants, a backward cap, and a popular label communicate his admiration for rebellion and social defiance. He likes to talk about the "big-timers," the Crypts and Bloods, gangs that strike terror in the heart of his parents . . . and friends.

Even though this boy is only sixteen, his girlfriend has already had one abortion. This to him is a status symbol of sorts. The young man has the ideals and values of a culture of death. He is on his way to nowhere.

Get the picture?

Acedia is indifference bred from an aversion to and negation of things spiritual. William J. Bennett defines the term well as "undue concern for external affairs and worldly things . . . [and] an absence of zeal for divine things."[1] From this loss of transcendent and eternal values has sprung the current environment in which pleasure, indulgence, and vanity rule supreme.

The great Russian dissident and patriot Aleksandr Solzhenitsyn described our current dilemma of social acedia in these terms: "In the United States the difficulties are not a Minotaur or a dragon, not imprisonment, hard labor, death, government harassment, and censorship, but cupidity, boredom, sloppiness, indifference. Not the acts of a mighty all-pervading repressive government but the failure of a listless public to make use of the freedom that is its birthright."[2]

Our young devotee of alternative MTV music and raunchy rap lyrics is the walking embodiment of acedia. The personal problem of this young man is that banality has turned into destruction, the death of his soul.

The insightful English writer Dorothy Sayers adds to our definition of the term. "The sixth deadly sin is named by the Church acedia or sloth. In the world it calls itself tolerance; but in hell it is called despair. It is the accomplice of the other sins and their worst punishment. It is the sin that believes in nothing, cares for nothing, enjoys nothing, loves nothing, and remains alive only because there is nothing it would die for. We have known it far too well for many years. The only thing perhaps that we have not known about it is that it is a mortal sin."[3]

America is afflicted with a corrupted heart and a decadent mind. We are becoming decivilized. National tolerance is the camouflage for our loss of moral purpose, the illness called acedia.

A Culture of Death

Because our legal staffers are deeply committed Christians, we believe it is our task to bring hope into a despondent world. In Matthew 4:16 we are told that "the people who sat in darkness have seen a great light," and we know Jesus Christ is the light of the world. We are committed to fighting the darkness even if at times we can only light one little candle. Our warfare is against the very Prince of Darkness himself.

The *Wall Street Journal* recently clarified how serious the issues are. Since 1960, violent crime has increased by 560 percent; illegitimate births have escalated by 419 percent; divorce rates have quadrupled. In this same thirty-year period, the percentage of children living in single-parent homes tripled while teenage suicides rose by 200 percent.[4] These facts present every Christian with a profound challenge.

Paulina can help us get the problem in focus.

The young exchange student came to the United States from Poland recently to broaden her education. After being here only a short time, Paulina was shocked. She reported, "In Warsaw we would talk to friends after school, go home and eat with our parents, and then do four or five hours of homework. When I first came here, it was like going into a crazy world." Paulina found that adjustment meant more time going to Pizza Hut and watching TV and less time doing schoolwork. She quickly discovered a great many of her peers' values and behavior were unacceptable to her. Paulina had a growing awareness that something wasn't quite right in the society into which she had been transplanted. The Polish teenager concluded her reflections on adjustment to American life with the observation that the American lifestyle of leisure "is not a good thing to get used to."

Paulina is right! No one should become complacent about the escalating trends of disintegration we are facing. A society that accepts illicit sexual relationships, adolescent promiscuity, abortion, cheating, lying, stealing, prostitution, divorce, and now even murder is heading for the edge. Today death walks the streets.

Accepting the Challenge

We have felt the enormous pressure this society puts on those who object to this environment. The "PC police" are relentless, but we simply can't accept the intimidation.

U.S. Representative Henry Hyde put it well. "There is a representative fundamentalism extant in our country today, but it's not of the religious variety. It is the secular fundamentalism that the courts, the ACLU, People for the American Way, and many of our law schools are teaching."[5] The American Center for Law and Justice is locked in mortal combat with these forces. We are committed to opposing the tides of political correctness that are sweeping our nation. Our charter issues—pro-liberty, pro-life, pro-family—are particularly galling to the PC establishment, but we will not give in to their pressure. America's future depends in large part upon the outcome of this battle. Though it is not politically correct to save unborn babies, or protect traditional family values, or to stand for First Amendment liberties, we believe it must be done. Our vision for America includes a revitalization of the values upon which this country was founded. The Constitution is at stake.

The War Zone

What exactly is going on in the war zone? Since assuming office, President Clinton has authorized the allocation of federal funds to underwrite "medical research" on the unborn. One of the ghoulish research projects is brain-snatching. With forceps, the abortionist turns the baby in the womb, pulling the child into the mother's birth canal. With the baby's head still inside the mother, the abortionist forces scissors into the base of the child's skull and opens the scissors to enlarge the opening. A suction catheter is then inserted into the open wound and the baby's brains are sucked out. The dead child is then removed and made available for experimentation.[6]

Some medical experts believe that grafting fetal brain cells onto the brains of patients afflicted with Parkinson's disease will help "the brain increase its production of dopamine, a vital neuro-transmitter necessary for smooth muscle movement of which Parkinson's patients are severely deficient."[7] Similar procedures are being tried with people suffering from Alzheimer's disease, diabetes, and leukemia. This grisly work requires seven to sixteen fetal brains for each adult patient.

Equally distressing is Dr. William F. Colliton's conclusion about such research. He said, "There's not one scintilla of evidence of a cure for anything."[8]

Doctors have other uses for the unborn. Researchers are learning how to retrieve the ova of aborted female children, fertilize them, and implant them back in infertile adult women. Dr. Roger Godsen, an infertility specialist at the Edinburgh Medical School, has been perfecting this technique with mice. He predicts the procedure will be available to humans in three years.

Behold! A new business opportunity looms on the horizon!

Women can become intentionally pregnant in order to sell their aborted children's eggs.[9] After all, business is business.

Even Aldous Huxley's vision of a brave new world was not as sick or malicious as the so-called progressive politically correct are today. What frightening irony! Newborns that are the creation of mothers who were never born themselves. Hitler's Final Solution for the Jews was no less bizarre.

Death in the Nursery

One step leads to another. What was unthinkable yesterday becomes thinkable today and is practiced tomorrow. The next logical extension of abortion is infanticide.

If unborn infants can be terminated, why not use the same procedures immediately after delivery? Dr. Milton Heifetz, former chief of neurological surgery at a Los Angeles hospital, has no problem with the concept. In his book *The Right to Die,* he acknowledges regularly ending the lives of infants whose existence he considered lacking in salvageable value. If, in his opinion, the infant wouldn't live an adequately meaningful life, then death was the best alternative. He argues that the newborn has no more value than the fetus and consequently life can be ended at will. Heifetz asks, "Is life at birth more significant than at the second, fourth, or sixth month of pregnancy? It is not."[10]

Pro-abortionist philosopher Peter Singer echoed the doctor's sentiments. "The life of a newborn baby is of less value than the life of a pig, a dog, chimpanzee."[11] Joseph Fletcher, the philosopher who brought us situational ethics, agrees with carrying out the logical implications of these arguments. He says, "It is reasonable to describe infanticide as a post-natal abortion."[12]

Are we describing the scenario in a sci-fi story? No, the practice of infanticide is not rare today. One medical writer reports, "The decision to withhold or withdraw treatment from extremely sick, premature, and/or deformed newborns is probably being made at least once every day by anguished parents and doctors in one of the nation's more than 500 intensive care nurseries."[13] Dr. Alan Fleischman, director of the division of neonatology at New York City's Albert Einstein College of Medicine, remarks that infanticide is "extremely common, it happens every day."[14]

Nurseries and wombs *have* become dangerous places in which to live.

How does extermination work? Sometimes life-saving surgery or simply food and water are withheld. On other occasions antibiotic drugs to fight disease aren't administered or overdoses are given. Some infants are abandoned to the natural elements or suffocated. A few children survive only a few minutes, but many more linger for hours. Some struggle on for days. All suffer.

The process begins when someone determines that the infants aren't wanted. From that point on, the downhill slide is quick. "Their care will be expensive. They have survived an abortion. They will never walk. They will lead 'unproductive' lives. They might end up in an institution at state expense. Above all, children in the United States are likely to be unwanted if they will suffer some degree of mental impairment. When such children need something to keep them alive—a routine operation, antibiotics therapy, even food and water—they may not get it in an American hospital today."[15]

The culture of death is creeping toward every age group and gender, from all walks of life. The court-legalized abortion mentality is slowly but surely enshrining an anti-ethic of genocide of the helpless. Under the guise of mercy and compassion, the right-to-die movement is eroding our guarantees to existence.

From Juniors to Geriatrics

What can the termination generation anticipate will follow? Once the unborn and the very young are at jeopardy, the handicapped, deformed, and elderly plagued by expensive or time-consuming illnesses are next to go. As death quickly approaches, the most economic response is speedy execution. The name for such an ultimate solution is euthanasia.

Today euthanasia has generally come to mean one of two things. Often, the idea implies allowing a person to die by withholding or withdrawing life-sustaining treatment. In other cases, euthanasia involves the direct and intentional killing of a person either by himself (suicide) or by another (assisted suicide or mercy killing). The first definition is passive euthanasia; the second is active euthanasia.[16] Groups like the Hemlock Society and the Society for the Right to Die believe that the distinction between active and passive euthanasia is morally irrelevant and that both forms of euthanasia are morally permissible and should be legalized.

Derek Humphrey, co-founder and president of the Hemlock Society, made euthanasia popular in the eyes of many in the American public by writing *Let Me Die Before I Wake.* His next book, *Final Exit,* sold more than half a million copies in hardback and remained the number one nonfiction hardback on the *New York Times* best sellers list for eighteen weeks. When it first came out, the book sold out more rapidly than reprints could keep up. Such books have helped to increase dramatically the practice of euthanasia in the United States.

In 1990, a Gallup poll revealed 69 percent of those surveyed approved of voluntary active euthanasia if the patient or family requested it. In contrast, only 37 percent supported the view in 1947.[17] A similar poll conducted by *USA Today* indicated that 68 percent of those polled felt that terminally ill people should be allowed to end their lives.[18] Washington and California have entertained voter initiatives to legalize physician-assisted death for the terminally ill. New Hampshire, Maine, Iowa, Michigan, and Oregon have considered legislation to legalize certain kinds of euthanasia.

Neither terminal illness nor agonizing pain is the essential issue with "euthanasiacs." Between 1990 and 1993, Dr. Jack Kevorkian, Michigan's "Dr. Death," participated in twenty suicides. Many were seriously ill but not terminally ill or in horrible pain. The Michigan doctor believes people with paralysis, stroke, emphysema, or severe arthritis should be able to find a doctor to help them fulfill their wish to be put to death. Kevorkian says, "The highest principle in medical ethics—in any kind of ethics—is personal autonomy, self-determination. What counts is what the patient wants and judges to be a benefit or a value in his or her life."[19]

Kevorkian calls his "services" to the public "medicide." Although Kevorkian has been indicted a number of times, he vows to continue helping people end their lives. He angrily told a reporter, "What's the court got to do with medicine! . . . They are dictating how medicine should be practiced. You know the court is dominated by religion . . . 'Life is sanctity, this and that . . .' so what! Instead of intimidating me, I'm intimidating them!"[20]

The ACLJ stands ready to lock arms with the people of light and life to stop the erosion of human worth. The erosion came one small step at a time. The Kevorkians of the world are not the first step. They are already the fifth or sixth step toward a society that sanctions execution of the vulnerable. In twenty or thirty years another generation of Americans could emerge who accept Kevorkian's radically destructive ideas as their starting point. Should that occur, the distance between them and death camps would be a very short trip.

We believe the future is literally at stake! The truth is, the modern euthanasia crusade is no more motivated by authentic love and compassion than is the pro-abortion movement. The death of thirty million aborted babies and untold victims of infanticide testify that reality can't be changed by calling death "reproductive rights" or "self-deliverance."

Exorcising Our Communities

You can help us in this fight by standing against all expressions of indifference. We must not let our towns, villages, and cities become desensitized to suffering, pain, and death. You can insist in every possible forum that the values of Hollywood expressed in violence and the assumption of birth control by abortion are not the ideals of America's heartland. Now is the time to fight for traditional American values of goodness, kindness, and human worth.

By the same token, now is not the time for "Chicken Little" responses. We don't need more cynics running frantically around warning that the sky is falling. Once we understand the severity of the current state of affairs and articulate it accurately and fairly, we need to point the way out of darkness into the light. The very mission of the Christian church is to engage and transform the culture, not to retreat or panic. Our task is to hold up the sky and influence the culture with the hope of the good news of Jesus Christ.

No matter how tough the fight for life, no matter how many setbacks we face, we must never give up. Because the Giver of life is with us, we can win!

The opposite of acedia is ardor and affection for life.

CHAPTER 10

DON'T LET THE SMOKE GET IN YOUR EYES

BATTLES HAVE been won; battles have been lost. But the sheer magnitude of the body count in the war for life can easily distort perspective, causing some pro-lifers such pain that ultimate objectives are obscured. We must never lose sight of the fact that in the beginning and end Christians stand for the sanctity of life. In the heat and fury of battle, it's easy to get confused.

D.C. Project assembled a massive anti-abortion protest by Christian organizations, picketing abortion clinics in the area in 1989. Following all the right procedures, leaders signed contracts for use of an armory and an auditorium as well as coordinating activities with police. Once the operation was public knowledge, NOW quickly filed a lawsuit to stop the project. One of the largest Washington law firms swung into attack. Jay and three other lawyers came to the defense, and NOW lost.

Not content with the first decision, attorneys for NOW filed two more lawsuits in Virginia and Maryland asking the courts to overrule the Washington decision by Judge Louis F. Oberdorfer. Jay and the team stayed up until 3:00 A.M. for four days, and when the dust had cleared NOW was defeated again. Jay had won.

Resistance didn't stop. The Washington City Council tried to thwart Judge Oberdorfer's decision by passing an emergency order to block the D.C. Project. Once again Jay's team countered and prevailed. Precedents were set, and protestors knew they didn't have to risk arrest at a clinic to be able to pass out leaflets portraying a realistic perspective of abortion. If the distribution was done on public property, they didn't risk arrest for trespassing.

Marching into Combat

The battle erupted again halfway across the country in Fargo, North Dakota, around the Fargo Women's Health Organization. The long and sophisticated title didn't conceal the fact that the clinic was an abortion business. Pro-life activist Kathleen Kirkeby and five friends were concerned about the presence of this clinic in their hometown and responded. Picketing focused on the residence of Jane Bovard, administrator of the abortion mill.

As the conflict escalated, city commissioners entered the conflict on February 1, 1993, by passing an ordinance aimed at stopping Kathy and the demonstrators. The new regulations forbade carrying written material or verbalizing protest within two hundred feet of a residence. The commissioners authorized the creation of "restricted picketing zones" where picketing was completely banned for a full year. The effect was to establish two restricted zones covering a full block where the pro-lifers had been picketing.

The ordinance was amended again on September 12, 1994. The ordinance defined picketing to include any activity attempting to persuade the public or to protest some action, attitude, or belief. Picketing was banned or limited for up to two years at a time. The city was clearly out to shut Kathy down.

Represented by Fargo attorney Peter Crary and ACLJ associate counsel Walter Weber, Kathy Kirkeby, David Habiger, Martin Wishnatsky, and Timothy Lingdren filed suit in federal court in June of 1993. They challenged the ordinance and the restricted areas and requested an injunction to halt enforcement of the regulation. Although the federal court initially denied the injunction, the pro-life attorneys appealed, and on April 20, 1995, the Eighth Circuit ruled that the city ordinance unconstitutionally restricted speech. The lower court was reversed on July 18, and the anti-picketing ordinance was ruled unconstitutional. The city of Fargo was permanently enjoined from enforcing the concept. Even though the city appealed back to the Eight Circuit, the pro-death forces had been stopped at the city gates.

Similar victory was achieved in St. Albans, Vermont. The Right to Refuse struggle began in January 1990, when a representative of the pro-abortion Vermont Catholics for Free Choice (VCFC) placed an order for membership forms with Regal Arts Press. Chuck and Susan Baker, owners of Regal Art, are strongly pro-life. As a matter of principle, the Bakers declined the business.

Linda Paquette, the VCFC representative, wouldn't leave the matter there. Astonishingly, she sued Regal Art Press. With the help of the ACLU, Paquette charged that Regal Art had violated a state anti-discrimination law by refusing her printing order on the basis of Paquette's "creed."

Vermont attorney Daniel J. Lynch and ACLJ attorney Walter M. Weber counterclaimed and asserted the Bakers' right to freedom of the press and freedom of conscience under both the U.S. and Vermont Constitutions. The Catholic League for Religious and Civil Rights as well as Christian Advocates Serving Evangelism joined the pro-life legal defense team.

On March 11, 1993, Jay Sekulow argued in the Superior Court for a summary judgment on the grounds that there was no discrimination. "This is not a case where the same service is provided to some people and not to others," he explained. "Regal Art Press refuses to print pro-abortion materials for *anyone.*" Jay cited the example of a kosher Jewish butcher who refused to trim ham for nonkosher Jews. "That's not discrimination," Jay maintained. "The butcher won't do that job for anyone else either. It makes no difference, therefore, if the butcher goes on to say that the customer should be ashamed of himself for not keeping kosher."[1]

On February 18, 1994, Superior Court Judge Linda Levitt

granted the defense motion. The state superior court threw out the religious discrimination suit. The judge commented in her ruling that it would be "bizarre and unreasonable" to accept Paquette's argument that the Vermont statute "forces one person to sacrifice its religious convictions by compelling it to help disseminate religious beliefs contrary to its own," supposedly in the name of religious equality. Of course, Linda Paquette appealed, and the case went to the Supreme Court and back to the Vermont Superior Court. In the end, Linda Paquette agreed that Regal Art Press had the right to refuse to print when the refusal was based on moral or religious opposition to the content.[2]

Chuck and Susan Baker had stood on conscience and prevailed.

The Death of Perspective

But some decisions have turned against us in recent days. The courts allowed the Racketeer Influenced and Corrupt Organizations Act (RICO) to be used against pro-life demonstrators. RICO was originally an attempt by the government to create laws enabling agencies like the FBI to catch the top leaders of the crime world. The intent was to expose the legitimate fronts covering up illegitimate schemes. The primary reason the act was applied to pro-lifers was that it allowed prosecutors to triple the amount of damages accessed against protestors. The U.S. Supreme Court's decision was definitely a pothole in the road for the pro-life movement.

While RICO was written to corral organized crime, it is now being used to impede an entire social protest movement.

Not only pro-lifers but all protesters are in danger of being labeled racketeers by this decision. The Court's opinion was a disaster, giving NOW a powerful weapon in their military arsenal. The death crowd can brand peaceful protesters, authors, publishers, and ardent advocates "racketeers."

Significant breakthrough in the right of protest came in Phoenix, Arizona. A city ordinance legislated a one-hundred-foot "shut-up" zone or "bubble zone" around abortion facilities. Peaceful protesting, counseling, and leafletting were illegal in this area. Six days later, Katherine Sabelko and Nancy Barto, pro-life demonstrators, challenged the ordinance with a lawsuit. Even though Planned Parenthood argued to protect the "bubble zone," Judge Stephen N. McName ruled for the two women. The bursting of the bubble gave new encouragement to the pro-lifers.

Unfortunately, the court of appeals upheld the ordinance, the decision was reversed, and the concept was allowed to stand. The new ruling was another "death of perspective" by court fiat. Joy turned to frustration and anger. The newly enacted Freedom of Access to Clinic Entrances Act (FACE) was designed for the sole purpose of controlling access to abortion clinic entrances. Use of FACE added to the protestors' outrage and hostility. Such a climate of despair can eventually twist the normally clear thinking of protestors.

The Gideon Project is an example of the unfortunate result of misplaced intentions. The Gideon Project's Matthew Goldsby and James Simmons thought God called them to a mission of destruction. On Christmas morning they destroyed an abortion clinic and the offices of two abortion-performing gynecologists with homemade pipe bombs. While Kay Wiggins,

Goldby's fiancée, called the bombing "a gift to Jesus on His birthday," a Pensacola jury called it terrorism and gave the two young men a ten-year prison term with five years of probation and ordered them to pay each gynecologist $353,073 in damages.

The recent killings of doctors and nurses in abortion clinics is further painful evidence of misguided intention. On June 5, 1995, the tragedy in Brookline, Massachusetts, where two clinic workers were intentionally killed was shocking. We anguished over the actions of Paul Hill, now convicted for the murder of an abortion doctor and a clinic volunteer. In these incidents, balanced perspective became another victim in the abortion battle. Despair turned into confusion.

Pro-Life Is Not Pro-Death

We are often asked, "If abortion is murder, is it right to kill abortionists?"

As an advocate of the pro-life movement for more than two-decades, Keith emphatically answers no. He affirms that life is sacred from the womb to the tomb. Never, never should assault on or the killing of abortionists be condoned or sanctioned! The opposite of acedia is certainly not assault.

Moreover, when laws are ignored, civil chaos reigns. The result is always the cheapening of human life. Christians believe God has ordained government to uphold good and punish evil. Even when government fails, shirks responsibility, or promotes evil (as is now the case with abortion on demand), such failures do not give individuals the right to take the law into their own hands. Vengeance is never justice.

Self-proclaimed pro-life advocates defending the killing of abortionists have walked into a moral and ethical fog. Taking the life of an abortionist is no different from what the doctor does in terminating the unborn. Two wrongs never make a right.

Keith is clear. We don't need more violence or attempts to justify destructiveness. We've had enough killing in this century.

What is needed is more full-bodied acts of genuine Christian love and nonviolent protest. Such deeds will take genuine courage and conviction. Violence is a nonproductive shortcut that only aids the opposition.

In the wake of Paul Hill's actions, Planned Parenthood ran misleading ads in the *New York Times* accusing prominent churchmen of inciting terrorism. New York's John Cardinal O'Connor was cited as an example of clergy advocating killing by their statements. Planned Parenthood implied the words of Christian leaders trying to save the unborn were like bullets used to kill abortionists. Tasteless attempts to raise funds and frighten Americans. All thinking citizens have to reject this. Unfortunately, their criticism was made possible by the actions of a pro-life activist.

One problem with violence is the chain reaction it creates. Each deed prompts a response. For example, after an abortion doctor was killed, a shot was fired at a pro-life demonstrator in Louisiana. Attack quickly became a two-way street.

A Malchus Moment

A controversial pro-life activist sent Keith a postcard. "I read your comments regarding the shooting of the abortionist. Evidently dead babies don't matter, only a dead abortionist."

The postcard writer had missed the meaning of a very important incident in the life of our Lord. Surely, if there ever was a wrongful arrest and death of innocence, it was the seizure and crucifixion of Jesus. During Jesus' incarceration, Peter grabbed a sword and attacked the soldiers, slicing off the ear of Malchus, the servant of the high priest. Jesus rebuked the violence and restored the man's ear. His actions made an even stronger statement than his words.

The meaning of the name Malchus is "king, royal, to ascend to the throne." The servant's name implied secular governing authority. From the name and the context of the story, we can see that Peter's action was an effort to overthrow secular rule.

Equally fascinating is the fact that the severed ear was on the right side. In ancient times, the right ear was considered the source of hearing. Jesus' act of restoration clearly conveyed another profound message. The church's role is to speak truth to those who wield secular power and to seek to influence the exercise of power with eternal values. While the state should listen when the church speaks, acts of violence by Christian people silence the church's moral voice. Insane acts of violence marginalize the Christian message and feed the caricatures promoted by our enemies. Jesus healed Malchus's ear to restore balanced perspective lost in Peter's impetuous attack.

If Peter is considered a representative of the church and Malchus a representative of the state, the story of Jesus' arrest forever puts all attacks on secular rulers in a clear light. The state, not the church, has the power to wield the sword.[3] As the Church marshals her awesome resources to defend the innocent, every deed must be done within the proper boundaries of God-given authority and with respect for life.

The killing of abortion doctors presents us with another Malchus moment. These dangerous crossroads call us to choose life and reject aggression. Let those with ears hear!

What Can You Do?

Even in today's difficult climate you can exercise significant expressions of conviction. You do not need to back away from the enemy. Here are doors that are still open.

- *You can distribute written material on abortion on public streets and sidewalks.* In almost every conceivable circumstance, you have the right to express your view on any issue. Misguided bureaucrats cannot call distribution of leaflets "solicitation." The Supreme Court treats handing out flyers as an activity distinctly different from solicitation. Leafletting is a well-established mode of protected expression.

The Court has maintained handing out leaflets is unobtrusive because the recipient "need not ponder the contents of a leaflet or pamphlet in order mechanically to take it out of someone's hand."[4]

Long ago, the Supreme Court declared unconstitutional a city ordinance of prohibition to prevent litter.[5] The desire of a city to keep streets clean is of another order from the right of citizens to express a viewpoint. Cities must deal with people who litter as a separate group from those who leaflet.

- *You can express opposition to abortion and offer alternatives by going personally to the public areas around a clinic.* Several important issues must be kept in mind. Remember, there is a legal difference between the streets, sidewalks, and parks of a community and the private property owned by another citizen. The Supreme Court has said that streets, sidewalks, and parks "have immemorially been held in trust for the use of the public and, time out of time, have been used for purposes of assembly, communicating thoughts between citizens, and discussing public question."[6] These public areas have historically been places where citizens discuss and debate issues of public importance. You must make sure to stay within the bounds of public use by staying on community-owned streets, sidewalks, and parks.

Your right of public expression is not absolute. What is said and done must be in peace and good order. City councils and county commissions can regulate the "time, place, and manner of such activities." However, municipalities cannot use the "guise of regulation" to abridge or deny such rights.[7]

The FACE legislation has created a new barrier in the name of public safety that can limit normally guaranteed constitutional rights. The city can pass ordinances that create an enclave around an abortion clinic where protest is not allowed. You need to inquire if such a restriction exists. You are in legal jeopardy if you protest in the face of such ordinances or if a court order exists prohibiting protest in some form.

- *You can march around the city block where an abortion business is located, provided you have met proper re-*

quirements. Cities can impose reasonable regulations of time, place, and matter on speech activities. Permits for marching may be rightly required. However, cities that impose "prior restraints" bear a heavy burden to justify their use. They cannot justify imposing greater cost on marches by persons expressing unpopular viewpoints.

You should check with the police department or city manager's office for information before proceeding. If the requirements seem burdensome or inappropriate, seek out legal counsel to clarify whether the ordinance is constitutional.

- *At every possible opportunity, you must insist that killing is not healthcare.* We must oppose any form of public healthcare program that includes abortion. We must insist that the "euthanasiacs" recognize that no amount of technical, verbal window dressing can camouflage the fact that they are proposing nothing less than killing. No one can measure the scope of influence from one person's witness to such facts.

The hardest path may yet prove to be the most effective. Few historians remember why killing in the Colosseum in Rome ceased. The battle was not won by a victory of violence over violence. On the contrary, more than four centuries after Christianity had made a significant impact on Rome, orchestrated killing continued with gladiators hacking each other to death each week.

One Sunday afternoon, a holy man came to town from his solitary desert prayer hermitage. Deeply burdened by the spectacle of death, Telemachus wandered into the arena. He leaped into the pit, stepping between two combatants, and demanded an end to the killing. The callous crowd laughed, and the gladiators tossed the monk aside, but the holy man was undaunted. Once more, he intervened, crying out for an end to the orgy of death.

"Run him through," someone yelled from the stands. The sword flashed, and the monk fell in the sand, his blood flowing around him. The sight of an innocent holy man killed for sport shocked the crowd to their senses. People began stealing away. One here . . . then another . . . then another . . . until the great amphitheater emptied, never to fill again. The integrity and courage of one holy man changed the mind of Rome.

What can you do? Never retreat. What may seem a personal defeat can be the prelude to the greatest victory. Good Fridays always precede Easter mornings. From Telemachus to Martin Luther King, Jr., the courageous have ultimately reshaped the world regardless of how fierce the struggle.

Just don't let the smoke get in your eyes.

CHAPTER 11

THE GOSPEL ON MAIN STREET

IN THE apostle Paul's day the marketplace was small and compact, and no one cared what went on as long as business wasn't interrupted. The preaching and discussion of new religious ideas was a novel diversion from the monotony of arguing over the lowest price of a bargain. Today the marketplace is vast, extending from world trade centers to the Internet. The unsophisticated days of a bearded little man sitting on a rug offering a simple clay pot to the best bidder disappeared with the hope that camels might be a nonpolluting means of public mass transportation.

Contemporary business involves zoning ordinances, federal legislation, union agreements, and government grants. Disinterest in what people believe has turned into passionate crusades to silence any witness to the gospel. Nothing is simple, and few employer-employee actions are without significant ramifications. Unfortunately, we cannot assume the regulators have the best interest of Christians at heart. On a warm March day in 1995, Pamela Rodriguez discovered this truth the hard way.

Pamela was an eligibility worker for Social Services in Los Angeles. As a Christian, she is opposed to engaging in any conduct that knowingly results in abortion. When a young Mexican national woman came in requesting a Medi-Cal card and approval for an abortion, Pamela was confronted with a personal decision. Medi-Cal cards entitle even alien holders to obtain a taxpayer-paid abortion in California. Four to five months pregnant, the woman wanted Pamela to assist her in starting a process that would end in the death of her unborn child. Pamela's personal convictions would not allow her to be part of facilitating an abortion, so Pamela was just going to send the women on to the next worker. Other employees indicated that they would do the task for her.

Pamela said, "I didn't want to participate in an abortion even though I wasn't personally doing the abortion myself. I felt that I *was* personally involved by giving her the card, and I didn't want to have any part of that. I went to the supervisor."

However, supervisor Bryan Logan wouldn't allow anyone else but Pamela to complete the assignment. The superior bore down, lecturing that Pamela's "personal views" couldn't interfere with her work. Logan warned Pamela to fill out the card or face a charge of insubordination, resulting in termination of employment.

Pamela's next step was to go up the administrative ladder to the deputy district director. She appealed to her deputy for transfer of the case. She remembers, "I tried to stand my ground. I told her, 'This is my belief. I don't want to be involved.' Deputy Marva Posey pounded the table and said 'You will issue this card.' . . . It caught me by surprise. So I said, 'Fine, I'll issue.' But I told her, 'I'm letting you know now I'm doing this under duress.'"

After being threatened with termination, Pamela issued the Medi-Cal card. Apparently she was being used as an example to others who might appeal to conscience. Pamela contacted the ACLJ seeking help.

Keith remembers thinking, "The new architects of tolerance are completely intolerant. In the name of openness, they shut out all disagreement. Title VII protects people in Pamela's predicament. She can't be made to act against her conscience. The America Center will help Pamela face this struggle."

As a matter of fact, the Department of Justice stands behind Title VII, which requires employers to provide "reasonable accommodation" to people like Pamela when there is conflict with their religious convictions. The employer was forcing a Christian employee into a position that violated her constitutional right to free exercise of religion.

In May 1995, the ACLJ filed suit in federal court, charging that the Department of Public Social Services violated Title

VII of the Civil Rights Act of 1964, the Free Exercise of Religion Clause and the Free Speech Clause of the First Amendment of the U.S. Constitution, and the Religious Freedom Restoration Act (RFRA).

Jay said, "Employees do not forfeit their religious beliefs when they enter the workplace. This is an issue about the accommodation of religious beliefs, not the endorsement of those beliefs. The constitutional rights of an employee must be protected—especially if it involves the expression of deeply held religious beliefs. Intolerance and discrimination in the workplace cannot and must not be tolerated."

By maintaining the courage of her convictions, Pamela is also acting on behalf of many of her fellow employees. Her lawsuit sought injunctive relief restraining the Department of Social Services from requiring her or other workers with the same convictions from having to assist in the abortion process. Pamela said, "As a born-again Christian, I cannot knowingly participate in the extermination of a life. Whereas, I am asking that this case be removed from my file."

The bottom line in Pamela's case is that Christian employees have failed to realize until now that they have the same rights and protections as the nonreligious employee. The ACLJ *is* making sure they know.

You need to know that religious discrimination encompasses loss of promotion because of one's Christian beliefs and certainly firing because of a stand or conviction. Employers cannot fail to give raises because an employee discusses religious convictions during free time such as lunch periods or coffee breaks. Christians can't be penalized for wearing religious clothing, T-shirts, or crosses. When problems arise in these areas, you have a right of recourse. The Equal Employment Opportunities Commission (EEOC) is the government agency responsible for investigating violations. You *do have* a court of appeal!

Friend or Foe?

Some Christians may read the foregoing with more than a bit of reservation. Alarm shot through the Christian community when the EEOC presented guidelines to stop religious discrimination in the workplace. The agency proposed that Bibles couldn't be out on desks and that Christian witness would be outlawed. Anyone remembering those headline stories may be amazed by the suggestion that the EEOC could be considered a friend.

Both the 700 Club and the ACLJ responded to their proposals and marshaled the faithful into solid opposition to these ideas. The switchboards of the EEOC were flooded with calls of outrage and protest. In turn, the ACLJ filed written notice explaining the meaning of their intentions. As a matter of fact, the EEOC was about to create religious segregation. Rather than addressing a problem of discrimination, they were trying to eradicate religion from the marketplace . . . quite the opposite of the reason for which the organization was created.

Under the combined pressure of the television audience and the legal response of our offices, the EEOC backed off and completely dropped the proposed regulations. The crisis was ended by our swift objections. The EEOC was kept within its proper boundaries.

Clean Air in Georgia

Pollution involves more than the Environmental Protection Agency (EPA) covers in their thick handbooks. Smog is a significant problem, but so is prurient behavior. The people of Rome, Georgia, didn't have trouble with the former, but they know a lot about the latter. In the summer of 1995, they found that their ability to proclaim the gospel with integrity was in jeopardy.

Nestled in northwest Georgia, the First Presbyterian Church of Rome, Georgia, has been faithfully sharing the gospel on Broad Street since 1856. The year General Sherman marched through Atlanta to the sea, First Presbyterian Church was building a sanctuary. From their inception, the church has known the meaning of the battle for the truth.

The faithfulness of the congregation resulted in steady growth through the many years. Additional properties were acquired, and the church's outreach expanded. The latest project has been the construction of a multipurpose facility, increasing family ministry to young adults, youth, and children in Rome.

Just as construction began, a nude dance bar opened up less than two hundred feet from the church. The Club Burlesque was a challenge to everything the church stood for and proclaimed. Obviously, the sexually explicit activities were totally incompatible and injurious to the mission of First Presbyterian Church.

Zoning normally controls encroachment and prohibits such public displays in proximity to a church. However, the owners of the club challenged the constitutionality of the zoning restrictions. The church had to enter the legal proceedings to defend their right to worship and minister effectively to area young people. Here's how the story unfolded.

Dr. Bill Flannigan had been in the ministry for thirty-five years and in Rome for four. One of his overriding concerns through the years had been national moral decay. As a pastor, Bill had often seen firsthand the destructive results of lust and pornography in destroying homes and individuals. He said, "We are deeply concerned with the erosion of morals, not only in the country, but in the community of Rome as well."

Consequently, the pastor was troubled when a church member, who was also a lawyer for the city, mentioned that the Club Burlesque was filing for an ordinance change that would put the club in the church's living room. Pastor Flannigan's response when the story hit the papers offers a model for other churches to follow.

The first step was to call a meeting of the elders. Reverend Flannigan asked his flock, "What can we do to preserve our spirituality and impact our community at the same time?" He knew the media thrived on calling churches "radicals," "Bible-thumpers," and similar polarizing names. The pastor wanted to take a far-reaching approach to the problem that would not cast the congregation in a negative light.

The leaders responded by forming a task force, which included two Christian lawyers. Reverend Flannigan remembers, "God's providence was at work from the beginning. One of the lawyers had just attended a Christian lawyers' seminar and heard Jay Sekulow speak. Our church had already sent mission money to the ACLJ. Divine timing was evident."

The task force called the church to prayer. The congregation interceded and asked the Lord to guide. The next step was to contact the ACLJ. Jay and Joel Thornton quickly came to Rome to talk with Bill and the church leaders. After initial conversations, the ACLJ joined Reverend Flannigan and the First Presbyterian Church of Rome in the battle to protect their neighborhood. The Christian lawyers of Rome were armed with the latest and most comprehensive data informing them of their full rights. Bill Flannigan remembers, "I was immediately impressed with the fact that Jay and Joel were godly men who had come to stand with us. In the beginning, I felt like Elijah alone, frightened and outnumbered by the prophets of Baal. Then God showed me through Jay and Joel there were seven thousand out there who hadn't bent the knee to the Baals. These men had the legal expertise average laymen don't have. There was no offensive picketing, shouting, just hard factually nose-to-nose dealing with legal issues."

The next step was to keep the congregation well informed. As information came from the ACLJ, it was passed on to the prayer warriors. People knew what was happening.

When the day of the court hearing came, Pastor Flannigan was far more nervous than he was in the pulpit on Sunday mornings. As he watched Jay present the facts in a straightforward, forceful fashion, he relaxed. In short order, the judge ruled to keep the ordinance intact as it was. A restraining order was placed against the club. The church had won!

The Ripple Effect

The Presbyterian congregation received tremendous encouragement from their victory. Already in the midst of a significant revival from the impact of Promisekeepers, young adults were coming to expect God to act when the congregation prayed. The judge's ruling was tangible evidence that confirmed their faith. But the results didn't stop there.

The lawyer for the Club Burlesque made a very interesting comment in print. The opposition admitted they couldn't prevail against a local church taking such a forceful stand or overcome the strength of the ACLJ.

First Presbyterian received numerous letters from other churches in distant communities thanking them for their action. Their legal victory gave these other groups hope for similar struggles.

New precedents were set for unified community action, which had immediate benefit. A short time later, a Chevron station in Rome applied for a permit to sell alcohol. The quick-stop station was much closer to a Roman Catholic church than the ordinances allowed, so the station sought a variance. The Catholic priest was troubled.

When the priest called on First Presbyterian Church for help, Pastor Flannigan sent four elders and the associate pastor to the city commissioners' hearing to stand with their Roman Catholic brothers and sisters. The word was already on the streets that the vote would be close and could be in favor of beer sales.

Presbyterian elder and retired Christian lawyer Charles Timbrel gave an impassioned plea to enforce the ordinance. He made it clear that Presbyterians were standing with the Roman Catholics. When he concluded, the commission voted unanimously to deny the request of the Chevron station.

From Mars Hill to Main Street

Let's go back to the marketplace in the apostle Paul's day for some instructive insight on how to proceed on Main Street America. True, Paul didn't have to contend with the ACLU or the EPA, but he still can give us important direction in the current climate of regulatory gridlock. Take a second look at what happened one afternoon in downtown Athens.

After a fairly hasty retreat from Berea, Paul landed in the historic Greek capitol. His fiery defense of the faith had gotten him close to a "disturbing the peace" charge up north. Once in Athens, Paul went straight to the marketplace and set up shop teaching and preaching as he did everywhere. The Epicureans and Stoics soon took note of his unusual message. Intrigued by the proclamation of the resurrection of Jesus, they invited Paul up to the Areopagus for a full-fledged discussion and debate.[1]

Of course, the critical, argumentative Greeks were more interested in a good debate than a step of faith. However, some listeners were definitely moved. Paul recognized the city was filled with statues of idols and seized on these objects as a means to make cultural analogies, comparing the Greek pantheon and the Christian God. He preached that Jesus was the end of their search for truth and a divinity to cover every situation. Dionysius the Areopagite and a woman named Damaris as well as others believed. Main Street proved to be a profitable place for evangelism.

Paul's visit to Athens forever provided a model for Christian witness. He demonstrated that civic problems must be viewed as ecclesiastical possibilities. We can't let the hecklers and detractors keep us from fulfilling the Great Commission in the town square of every community in the world.

Sure, camels have been replaced by Cougars and Jaguars as modes of transportation. The forum of the Areopagus has become today's media, but Paul still left us solid guidelines for taking the gospel to Main Street:

- Don't be intimidated by the opposition. If they didn't like Jesus, they won't be crazy about us. Hostility comes with the territory.
- Don't be afraid to stand your ground. Resistance today doesn't obscure the promise of victory tomorrow. No one knows what God may yet choose to use to His glory.
- Don't smash idols; replace them. You don't have to fight over the "hunks of junk" to show the superiority of the risen Christ to the relics of the pipe dreams of disillusioned people.
- Find their cultural openness and read it accurately. The Greeks were God-hungry people. Paul offered them a better diet. While some resisted, others agreed. One never knows who will be touched by the honest courage of a faithful witness.
- Offer them the Gospel of Life to replace their religion of death. Inanimate statues are no substitute for the One who is the Way, the Truth, and *the Life.* Sooner or later when death calls at their home, they will want to know more about the Great Physician who was the only one who ever offered the dying resurrection.

Pamela Rodriguez was following this model in her witness to life. While the issue was not a straightforward gospel message, her response was a faithful cultural refutation of the idols of hedonism and self-indulgence in a culture of death. As the "brethren" at Berea surrounded Paul, as Dionysius and Damaris stood with Paul, so the ACLJ stood with Pamela.

Fighting Religious Discrimination in the Workplace

What can you do to fight religious discrimination? The cases of Pamela Rodriguez and Reverend Bill Flannigan can help us. Their courage makes it clear that any one of us can make a difference. Here are the answers to a few critical questions.

Q. *What should you do when you are the victim of religious prejudice?*

A. *Like sexual discrimination, religious discrimination is often hard to describe and define. Because proving religious discrimination can be complicated, the ACLJ recommends that you carefully document problems in preparing a claim. Keep a history of events, times, and places as well as exact content of discussions. While Christians are warned that those who desire to live godly lives will be persecuted, we should also understand that the law offers us certain boundaries of protection. Take the covering the law offers. You are entitled to your rights.*

The EEOC remains one of the most effective sources of assistance you have. This agency investigates claims of racial, sexual, and religious discrimination in the workplace. Many states have few laws protecting your right to work in a discrimination-free environment; thus the EEOC is often your only real remedy if you have been denied a promotion or fired because of religious beliefs.

Q. *What protection does the EEOC offer me?*

A. *Title VII of the Civil Rights Act of 1964. EEOC polices the workplace, enforcing legislation that prohibits discrimination based on race, color, sex, religion, or national origin. You are legally covered by this act.*

Q. *How can I use this opportunity?*

A. You must file a complaint. The process for filing a complaint is very tedious. You start by filing with the state or federal branch of the EEOC. This step must be taken before you can file a federal lawsuit in a federal district court.

Q. *Are there time requirements?*

A. Yes. In states where there is an anti-discrimination law and a state agency authorized to act on your behalf, you must file with the EEOC within three hundred days of the discriminatory act. If you file with the state EEOC first, you may request a review of their decision to the federal EEOC within sixty days. If there is no state agency with the proper authority, you must file a complaint with the EEOC within one hundred days of the problem.

Q. *What's the rush?*

A. The need for expeditious action. The theory is that constitutional rights violations are so grievous that legitimate complaints will be made quickly. In addition, the longer you wait to file a complaint, the harder the violation is to prove. As time passes, witnesses are harder to locate,

memories blur, and people lose motivation to testify because of promotions.

Q. ***What will the EEOC do?***

A. ***Start an investigation process. The agency will notify your employer or former employer of the charges. They will interview witnesses and request information. Witnesses will be interviewed. The EEOC will attempt to persuade the employer to eliminate the source of the problem and correct violations of Title VII. They will seek your lost benefits or wages. If nothing is accomplished and your claim is found to be valid, EEOC may file a lawsuit. After receiving notice of the "right-to-sue" from EEOC, you must file a private lawsuit or will lose your right to file a legal claim.***

Remember: You must request the "right-to-sue" letter from EEOC, as they will not send it automatically. In addition, you must prove your claims.

Q. ***How do I proceed?***

A. ***To obtain the correct forms for filing a complaint, call 1-800-USA-EEOC.***

Keeping Main Street Open

Pastor Bill Flannigan told us he simply didn't have a clear idea how to proceed legally when the zoning issue arose. In the past, clergy have generally not been in the public legal battles that have become commonplace. Here are some of the things he learned about changing local laws.

Issues involving city councils and school boards are often

best handled by an attorney. Generally, these encounters require an in-depth knowledge of the law and how it works since municipal groups expect the same preparation that an attorney puts into developing a court case. Because the ACLJ has vast experience in these issues, we can send attorneys who already are aware of successful legal strategies. Often we are able to resolve serious problems without ever going to court.

While First Amendment freedoms must be protected, how the law is presented is important. The spokesperson must possess a wide range of skills, including abilities in legal research, negotiation, communications, and public relations. In addition, mindfulness of sensitive local issues is important. You can call on the ACLJ to help you formulate the best strategy for your particular situation.

Don't underestimate the significance of starting with your local boards and councils. You have more influence in your community than you probably think. Hometown groups are the first line of decision making. You have access to the immediate mechanisms for change. The heavy emphasis is on *local.* Most problems begin with a local, not state, regulation. Student problems as well as issues with city parks and sidewalks start within the community. *You are an important component in the local setting.*

Generally, local boards and councils are elected. The democratic process makes elected officials very sensitive to an unhappy public. Alienation of one's constituency isn't the way to get reelected.

Because local officials don't relish court battles, whenever possible, they will attempt to resolve issues. Compromise is often in the air. These officials aren't interested in seeing taxpayers' money spent on litigation. If you can help them avoid a lawsuit, they may even rise up and call you blessed!

At no other level is government as directly responsive to the people as it is locally. When Presbyterian elder Charles Timbrel spoke in Rome, the tide of opinion changed. By warning the city commissioners of the strength of Christian opinion, he not only helped the Catholics, he saved the commissioners a considerable amount of future legal grief.

Paul's Example

Paul's debate at Mars Hill wasn't the only example the apostle gave us for how to respond in difficult civic situations.

The final showdown in Paul's confrontation with legal authorities came when his case was finally placed before Porcius Festus, the governor in Jerusalem. Even though his treatment had not been fair and Festus's interest and intentions were to appease and placate Paul's enemies, the apostle's defense was clear.

Paul appealed to the legal system of his day. "I stand at Caesar's judgment seat, where I ought to be judged. To the Jews I have done no wrong, as you very well know. For if I am an offender, or have committed anything deserving of death, I do not object to dying; but if there is nothing in these things of which these men accuse me, no one can deliver me to them. I appeal to Caesar."[2]

Paul demanded his rights as a Roman citizen. His example is a clear indication of the path we should follow. When we enter a courtroom, petition the EEOC, or address a city council, we should be true to the obligations of good Christian citizenship.

PART 3

The Future

CHAPTER 12

THE ROAD TO TOMORROW

LIZ CHARITY has always been concerned about the future. In her heart she carries a burning compassion for the tomorrows of young people. While working with teens in her local church, Liz sensed a special calling. She knew the future for many black young people in the inner city was strewn with social mines that could explode at any time, destroying their possibilities for personal fulfillment.

"I realized God put a special anointing on me for kids," Liz says. "The gospel and the church are central, but I wanted to develop the whole person. I wanted to help cultivate young people socially, physically, emotionally, as well as spiritually. I was interested in the whole person."

Elizabeth Harris Charity's dedication was channeled toward "high-risk" young people in downtown Richmond, Virginia. She started Youth Outreach Services (YOS) to make a difference in the future of troubled kids. Wanting to go far beyond the commitment of her church, Liz sought to bring citizens, private businesses, and local government into an alliance to help teenagers become employable. YOS created programs that focused the talents and resources of teachers, committed citizens, and business leaders into a unified approach helping young people in distress. Liz obtained a tax-exempt status and started the YOS vocation training center.

YOS quickly became so successful that a waiting list was necessary. As many as eighty teens stood in line to get a chance for a change in their lives. Students signed contracts pledging to put money back into YOS after they gained employment so other teens could be helped.

Recognizing the heart of the contemporary welfare problem, Liz Charity said of her work, "For the past five years, God has given me a vision by which the people of Virginia can take back their communities." She knew from firsthand experience the dilemma urban youngsters faced. For over half a decade, Liz had been effectively working with and ministering to the physical, emotional, and spiritual well-being of inner-city families. She had seen dramatic results. Lives were changed, relationships restored. Young people learned skills that would make them productive citizens.

Governor George Allen was so impressed that he provided

a grant of $69,000 from the Governor's Discretionary Fund. He said, "These young folks are our future and they have a tough way ahead of them." And that's when the trouble began.

Roadblocks from the Left

In typical fashion, the American Civil Liberties Union objected to public funding for Liz's organization. The ACLU asked the attorney general of Virginia to investigate "state funding of religious organizations." Once again social liberals were attempting to crush the spirit of renewal in their pursuit of religious cleansing.

Liz Charity's highly significant work came to a screeching halt. Under Virginia law, the government had to freeze the grant while an investigation was in progress. The office building was closed. An attempt at private welfare reform by citizens had been overturned by ACLU intervention.

ACLU executive director Kent Willis said, "The ACLU has no argument with the group's mission but with its funding from the government." He was simply not up on current law. The American Center for Law and Justice had filed a friend of the court brief the summer before in a Supreme Court case that had direct bearing. *Rosenberger v. the Rector and Visitors of the University of Virginia* set the stage for the court to overrule the specific contention of the ACLU that providing religious institutions financial support violated separation of church and state.

Ronald Rosenberger found himself the victim of similar discrimination while publishing a student-run Christian magazine, *Wide Awake,* which was circulated on the University of Virginia campus. University student activity funds were regularly doled out to 118 student groups and newspapers appearing around the school. University funds were provided for publications by a Muslim organization, a Gandhi peace group, animal rights advocates, and a homosexual/lesbian group. But, because Rosenberger's publication was Christian, funds were denied.

The staff of *Wide Awake* appealed to the student level of university government and was rejected. University officials also turned a deaf ear. When Rosenberger's team petitioned the federal court, they lost again. However, Ronald and his band of believers did not lose faith or hope. They took their case to the Supreme Court and won!

Writing for the majority of the Court, Justice Anthony M. Kennedy said, "Vital First Amendment speech principles are at stake here. We hold that the regulation invoked to deny [student fund] support, both in its terms and in its application to these [Christian students], is a denial of their right of free speech guaranteed by the First Amendment."[1]

Like Ronald Rosenberger, Liz Charity was a victim of religious discrimination practiced by groups attempting to remove Christian presence from public life. Letters from the ACLJ brought this disparity to the attention of all involved in the funding of Liz Charity's YOS program.

Interestingly enough, when the administrator of the grants from the governor's office was asked about the religious component in Youth Outreach Services, he replied, "If a place or organization has a religious aspect to it that is their right." Virginia's attorney general's office knew the Free Speech Clause protects organizations like YOS. Rights available to other citizens or groups cannot be denied to Christians simply because of their faith.

Without question, Liz Charity's Christian faith is a significant motivating force in her work. But Christians are not to be treated like second-class citizens simply because they have convictions and voice them. Justice William Brennan said in a similar case, "The Establishment Clause does not license government to treat religious people, or religious practices, as if they are subversive to American ideals, and therefore, subject to unique disabilities."[2]

When Jay contacted Elizabeth Charity at the closed Youth Outreach Services' building, a man in his sixties walked up. He looked Jay straight in the eyes and pleaded, "Jay Sekulow, you have to do something about this. We must have this facility opened up for our kids."

Jay assured the concerned man that the ACLJ Office of Governmental Affairs was already working with congressional leaders to ensure that religious institutions will not have to strip away their faith when reaching out to the needy. Our intervention helped Liz's work avoid getting bogged down in endless litigation. Rather than turn to the courts, the legal questions were channeled to the state attorney general's office. Jay wrote an appeal letter directly to Virginia governor George Allen.

In fact, our Religious Liberties Project is currently involved with the attorney general's staff to make sure that religious missions, ministries, and organizations are not denied the right to participate in grants. We believe our role will assist the attorney general's office in bringing tolerance for the Christian presence in the state of Virginia.

While waiting for the final opinion, Liz has written two books and continues to help kids. When her problems were featured on the *700 Club,* Liz was greatly encouraged by receiving a phone call from Texas. A viewer was inspired and wanted details on YOS to use as a model for a similar program. What was meant for evil was now being used for good.

Like Ronald Rosenberger, Liz has a message of hope and encouragement for Christians. She says, "Whatever you believe, don't back off." Elizabeth Harris Charity is one of our companions on the road to tomorrow.

For Liberty, Life, and Family

We have assembled Christian lawyers, thinkers, philosophers, apologists, and activists who recognize the signs of the times and seek to develop a response that will bring intellectual conversion to a secularized America—and even beyond to a decimated Western civilization.

In order to accomplish such a monumental task, new thinking and thinkers must rise up and give a contemporary voice to classical Christian thought. The alliance must cross confessional, racial, socioeconomic, gender, and political lines to bear witness to the universality of the Christian message. The answer has already taken shape in the ecumenical nature of the ACLJ. Staff members of evangelical, messianic Jewish, and classical orthodox Catholic persuasion have united in common cause to bring the truth of Jesus Christ to bear on national life.

We are committed to recapturing the mind and culture of America, because the future is at stake. The very survival of ordered liberty, the sanctity of all life, and the value of the family are in the balance.

The goal of the ACLJ is well expressed in the accord drafted largely by Charles Colson and Richard John Neuhaus. "Evangelicals and Catholics Together: The Christian Mission in the Third Millennium" reads:

> Together we contend for the truth that politics, law and culture must be secured by moral truth. With the Founders of the American experiment, we declare, "We hold these truths." With them, we hold that this constitutional order is composed not just of rules and procedures but is most essentially a moral experiment. With them, we hold that only a virtuous people can be free and just, and that virtue is secured by religion. To propose that securing civil virtue is the purpose of religion is blasphemous. To deny that securing civil virtue is a benefit of religion is blindness.[3]

Common Cause

Keith's significant work, *A House United,* describes the basis on which evangelicals and Catholics can come together under the common banner of Christ. Important doctrinal and ideological distinctives do not proclude making common cause in legal, cultural, and policy initiatives.

Just as the Allies in World War II needed one another to overcome the armies of destruction that threatened the world, so also Catholics and Protestants need each other to push back the darkness of secularization, dehumanization, racism, and the other forces opposed to moral and ordered liberty. Together we are stronger.

Throughout our common Judeo-Christian history, we have received a tremendous family legacy. Our differences must not obscure the overwhelming commonalities that bind us together. The "Evangelicals and Catholics Together" accord said:

> Together we search for a fuller and clearer understanding of God's revelation in Christ and his will for his disciples. Because of the limitations of human reason and language, which limitations are compounded by sin, we cannot understand completely the transcendent reality of God and his ways. . . . We now search together in confident reliance upon God's self-revelation in Jesus Christ, the sure testimony of Holy Scripture, and the promise of the Spirit to his church. In this search to understand the truth more fully and clearly, we need one another.[4]

The operative word is *common.* Consider the vastness of what we share. The Bible is the treasure chest of our common faith. We hold a common history springing from one root—the root of Jesse—the offspring of David. Our doctrines arising from scripture are expressed and formalized in common creeds. Of course, most significant of all is our common Savior, Jesus the Christ. Our Lord is destroying all separating walls of ignorance and hostility and calling us into a common mission of proclaiming and teaching the gospel.

We seek the establishment of such an order on behalf of life before birth and at the end among the elderly and the ill; in Congress, the courts, and communities; as well as on behalf of the family in all of its expressions.

The Foundations of the Future

The history of Western civilization has been shaped by small bands of Christians committed to extending the light of God's glorious truth into every dark place in society. The few laid the foundation blocks on which the future was built.

In the fifth century, St. Benedict and his sister St. Scholastica confronted the immorality of the declining Roman Empire by forming a small community in the northern Italian mountains dedicated to prayer and fasting. Years later when Rome needed great men and women of insight and vision, they appeared out of St. Benedict's community. They came back down from the high mountains to begin the task of recivilizing the Roman world.

Centuries later, similar great Christians founded universities in three strategic cities: Bologna, Italy; Paris, France; and Oxford, England. As the first millennium drew to a close, communities sprang up around these centers of thought and inquiry. Every area of Western civilization was molded by their contributions in law, government, religion, education, the sciences, and family life. As other colleges were founded, Europe began to ripen into the modern age. The church had established the foundations and provided the pillars on which the whole culture would stand.

As we come to the end of the second millennium, our cultural challenges are no less significant. The architects of death are determined to destroy these contributions of the past and build on a new basis. If they succeed, our cities are in no less danger than when the Huns and Vandals descended on the gates of Rome to sack the treasures amassed across the centuries. The tasks of the ACLJ are to expose these destructive strategies and dispel the darkness.

The cost of failing is too high for us even to consider. The forces pushing "religious cleansing" confront us with the specter of social death. Almost two decades ago, the Russian author and prison-camp survivor Aleksandr Solzhenitsyn saw the same truth. Speaking to the United States Congress, he prophetically advised the American people, "Very soon, only too soon, your country will stand in need of not just exceptional men, but of great men. Find them in your soul. Find them in your hearts. Find them in the depths of your country."

The hope of tomorrow is to be found in the storehouse of yesterday. The national soul is kept there. From the cultural treasures of the past are the promises for future generations. The belief in the sacredness of life, a zeal for liberty, the strength of the two-parent, marriage-bound family, the society-building principle of offering aid and giving mutual support, the concept of self-evident truths—each is a component for building the future.

Like St. Benedict, we need to raise up a generation of parents, public servants, judges, teachers, pastors, writers, prophets, evangelists, and apologists who can confront the present cultural apostasy with the great truths of our faith.

Reflections

Keith's vision of these possibilities began during his two years of monastic life in the Pecos Benedictine community more than twenty years ago. The monastery's founder, Abbot David Gaerats, had a dream of the power of a faithful community of men and women given both to the cultivation of the interior life and to a passionate concern for the conversion of society. During his time as a part of the Benedictine discipline, Keith realized that men and women bonded together in love and service could change every form of social ill by upholding each other in love and prayer as they worked together for change.

Abbot David modeled the transforming power of the interior life. He spoke of an intimacy with Jesus that made people hunger for God. Keith's exploration of these promises led him through the writings of Christian saints like St. Francis of Assisi and St. Benedict. He learned to live out the continual repetition of the Jesus Prayer—"Lord Jesus Christ, son of God, have mercy upon us"—as a way of praying without ceasing. At the time, he didn't realize the quiet retreat setting in the New Mexico mountains around Pecos was actually preparing him for the rough-and-tumble arena of the world of litigation.

St. Benedict's way was always to challenge the brothers in their hermitages with the reminder that a monastery was not a place in which to hide from the world. Keith quickly learned the meaning of Thomas Merton's admonition not to leave the world outside but to bring it with you into the monastery. In addition, Abbot David taught Keith that you don't park your brains when you enter the way of faith. Years later these ideals are still shaping Keith's plans for the future.

Hope remains the driving motivation behind Keith's expectation for the future. Keith contends that Richard John Neuhaus's ideal of a "reconfessionalized ecumenism" will bring all segments of Christian witness into unified focus. The next century will witness a rebirth of Christian unity and renewed social action. Keith believes the ACLJ will be marching in this procession.

The Next Step

We have already launched seven major projects to achieve our goals for the ACLJ. Each endeavor has ramifications for you and your family's future. As exciting as the past has been, the days ahead are filled with even greater promise. Here are some of the components for the recasting of the next millennium.

The Liberty Project will fight to restore the American tradition guaranteeing freedom of religious expression and discussion in the marketplace of ideas.

An example is currently unfolding in Phoenix, Arizona. The city owns public transit buses and allows advertising on the buses. However, the city practiced content and viewpoint discrimination by excluding religious advertising. In the past, the city has allowed controversial messages promoting gay rights and condom usage while still refusing rental space to the Children of the Rosary organization supporting life. The ACLJ is contending for the group's rights.

Similarly, the city of Tucson will not allow music with singing and proselytizing while distributing food to the poor, obviously an outrageous restriction on evangelism. Prohibiting a gospel message while giving food to the needy is an obnoxious form of censorship. The Liberty Project exists to confront these assaults on religious expression.

The Life Project seeks to secure respect and legal protection for all human life—from natural birth to natural death. Both the dignity of life and the right to existence must again become bedrock principles of law and public policy.

Such ends were accomplished during the struggle to pass the ban on partial-birth abortions. We worked with Congressman Charles Canady to obtain grassroots support for this significant legislation. Congress overwhelmingly passed the bill. Our next step is to fight for restrictions on late-term abortions.

The ACLJ is currently challenging the Freedom of Access to Clinic Entrances Act (FACE) and has filed additional briefings under the Commerce clause. We are hopeful of reversing this destructive legislation.

The Family Project is designed to reestablish the primacy of the two-parent, marriage-bound family as the primary social organization. The home is the first government, the first school, the first church, and the first economic institution. It should be treated as such.

The ACLJ will continue to battle attempts by the homosexual community to give legitimate status to immoral relationships. Attorney General Michael Boweres was sued for refusing to hire a lesbian who participated in a gay marriage ceremony. We are filing a brief on his behalf.

Social services worker Jane Howard was discriminated against by fellow employees after she expressed the opinion that homosexuality was a violation of biblical standards. The executive director for Store Front Youth Action reprimanded Howard and said her ideals conflicted with the views of the agency. After ACLJ intervention, the director retreated. Such victories protect Christians' right to their beliefs while defending the family as the basic unit in society.

The recent debate and development of the telecommunications law was an opportunity for the ACLJ Office of Government Affairs to help in drafting language for legislation that outlawed the transmission of indecent and other sexually explicit materials over computer networks. ACLJ staffers also helped defend the bill.

The Education Project will fight to guard against an ever-encroaching national education bureaucracy that seeks to undermine the historic concept of "public" education. Bureaucrats are opposed to the idea that local schools belong to the people, are governed by the immediate community, and should be influenced by the parents. We intend to uphold parents seeking final determination of the education of their own children and grant to them a full range of options including public, private, religious, and home schooling.

Tammy Gunnell's problems with the University of Oregon illustrate the Education Project at work. Tammy applied for a voucher from the university that would credit up to 45 percent of child-care costs for single parents attending classes. Her application was denied because her child attended a Christian child-care center. The ACLJ sent a demand letter clarifying the application of equal access policy. An interim agreement with the university was quickly reached, and Tammy received a check for child-care costs retroactive to the beginning of the school year. She also was granted extended child care. ACLJ attorneys helped draft the university's new policy.

The Government Project will assist the requests of legislators seeking resources in drafting "faith and family friendly" legislation. Staff members will assist in monitoring the government's treatment of people of faith at the federal, state, and local levels.

Recently, Congress defined and declared indecency prohibitions affecting the airwaves of both radio and television. Once these regulations were challenged, the ACLJ filed briefs before the United States Supreme Court to defend the legislation. Our Office of Government Affairs sought the support of more than ninety Congressmen. Our positive relationships on Capitol Hill are hopeful signs for future action. In a similar way, the ACLJ is working with Senator Charles Grassley on the Parental Rights and Responsibilities Act, which would require government agencies, including school districts, to have clear, well-defined, and legislatively mandated reasons before policies are adopted. We want to stop arbitrary intervention to create social change.

The Minority Project offers support for the cause of civil and natural rights of all Americans by enhancing minority economic, educational, and political development for full participation in a free society. We will seek traditional constitutional values of life, liberty, property, limited government, and equal justice under law for all minorities.

The Economics Project is designed to defend the free enterprise system against the tyranny of overregulation and to oppose government usurpation of economic competition. The project is committed to the support of capitalism with a conscience, an economic system infused with moral and religious values and principles.

Digital Fish, a for-profit software company, got caught in the net of prejudicial government regulations. The Economics Project came to their aid. Digital Fish develops market computer products with Christian themes for home use, but the company is not part of any church organization.

The company's full line spans a wide variety of categories, including children's learning helps, references, and games. Their application for a small business loan was quickly approved by Sterling Bank and forwarded to the Small Business Administration (SBA) for approval. SBA rejected the loan on eligibility grounds because products were being developed for Christians. In turn, the ACLJ prepared a lawsuit against the Small Business Administration.

The Small Business Administration's response was to approve the application and to stop denying Christians equal access to the marketplace of ideas. Our lawsuit was intended to ensure Digital Fish equal opportunity under the law.

Where do you fit in this picture?

Your Place

In the preceding chapters we have shared some of the stories of the men and women, the boys and girls, who refused to accept the status quo and wouldn't allow injustice to stand unchallenged. Without their resistance and fortitude, nothing would have changed.

We challenge you to join with us by refusing to honor the Trojan horses secularists have rolled into our cities and school auditoriums and parked in front of our churches. You become part of the team by refusing to accept discrimination in your office or censorship in the town square. When you refuse to be intimidated, your integrity sets the stage for legal action that challenges the climate in all of our communities.

The Shape of Tomorrow

When the presidential guidelines on religion in the schools came out, Jay and Keith expected the old confrontations to disappear. To the contrary, the demands on the ACLJ increased. As the word got out to the Christian community, more and more people were standing up for their rights. Reflecting on this trend, Jay says, "The future will be determined by the degree to which the church is willing to stand up and fight. We need to see a generation of parents, pastors, youth workers, and teachers who will nurture our kids in the meaning of this new legal climate. Our children are our future."

Jay's view of his place in the coming day is conditioned by his own past struggles. During the early days of his career, Jay did quite well. His first firm grew quickly and soon had nine lawyers, two full-time certified public accountants, and three paralegals. He branched out into the construction business, which soon occupied five floors of a downtown office building.

Unexpectedly, the tax codes changed and Jay's empire crumbled. From successful young lawyer, Jay went to the bottom, losing business, house, fortune, and even his car.

One evening, sitting alone and facing the pain of failure, Jay prayed that God would grant him one more chance to do something of significance for the Lord. A short while later the Los Angeles Jews for Jesus airport Supreme Court case emerged. The rest is history.

Jay says, "I remember everyday where I came from. My successes are not the result of what I have done but what God has done through me. My story is the experience of defeat turned into victory by God's grace. I have seen the power of the gospel firsthand. I want to do everything I can to make sure the avenues of communication remain open for the proclamation of the gospel. To that end, my work in our nation's courts, in the halls of Congress, and even in the media is to do whatever I can to assure open access to the ultimate message of hope."

What drives Jay today? His faith in God and then in his family. Next to his faith, Pam and his children take precedence over all other considerations. He states emphatically, "If Christians don't stand up, my children will inherit a world that will be impossible to get back on track. My quest is to create a better world for the kids."

Jay Sekulow believes his future role will be to help create a platform for coming generations to reclaim our culture and protect the future. The law is coming into place. The next step is to accomplish nationwide recognition of the primacy of religious freedom. It won't be easy, but the job *can* be done.

Claiming the Future

As a dedicated Christian apologist, Keith Fournier is convinced the third millennium requires a new generation that can present the classical Christian message as a solution for a decimated Western civilization. His experience in the practice of law, his writing, and his public proclamation of the gospel convince him of the vital importance of liberty, the defense of life, and the protection of the family.

Yet, when asked what is most significant in his life, he, too, places his family at the top of the list. "I know my first and primary vocation is to be husband and father. The family is the domestic church, the key to our future. Rather than curse the darkness, it is time to light a candle. We need to proclaim the hope and vision which animated our ancestors to build this nation, 'conceived in liberty and dedicated to the proposition that all men are created equal.' The future need not be met with fear, but with faith."

Together Jay and Keith have decided to be part of the solution, not just struggle with current problems. They hope to be numbered among the generation that rebuilds a culture of life where families thrive and liberty again shines a beacon of hope.

Most often known for saying, "All that is necessary for evil to triumph is for good men to do nothing," Edmund Burke spoke of "little platoons," families, churches, neighborhoods, community groups, charities, and voluntary associations, through whom God's work is best accomplished. We stand at a millennial moment. We are called to become "little platoons" taking action and responsibility to do God's work throughout our nation. Jay and Keith have hope for the future because the ACLJ and many similar groups across the country are doing something to prevent the triumph of evil. They invite you to share their vision.

"For the vision is yet for an appointed time, but at the end it shall speak, and not lie: though it tarry, wait for it; because it will surely come, it will not tarry."

Remarks by President Bill Clinton on Religious Liberty in America

James Madison High School
Vienna, Virginia
10:56 A.M. EDT

Thank you, Secretary Riley, for the introduction, but more for your outstanding leadership of the Department of Education and the work you have done not only to increase the investment of our country in education, but also to lift the quality and the standards of education and to deal forthrightly with some of the more difficult, but important issues in education that go to the heart of the character of the young people we build in our country.

Superintendent Spillane, congratulations on your award

and the work you are doing here in this district. Dr. Clark, Ms. Lubetkin. To Danny Murphy, I thought he gave such a good speech I could imagine him on a lot of platforms in the years ahead. (Laughter.) He did a very fine job.

Mayor Robinson, and to the Board of Supervisors—Chair Katherine Hanley, and to all the religious leaders, parents, students who are here; the teachers; and especially to the James Madison teachers, thank you for coming today.

Last week at my alma mater, Georgetown, I had a chance to do something that I hope to do more often as president, to have a genuine conversation with the American people about the best way for us to move forward as a nation and to resolve some of the great questions that are nagging at us today. I believe, as I have said repeatedly, that our nation faces two great challenges: first of all, to restore the American dream of opportunity, and the American tradition of responsibility; and second, to bring our country together amidst all of our diversity in a stronger community so that we can find common ground and move forward together.

In my first two years as president I worked harder on the first question, how to get the economy going, how to deal with the specific problems of the country, how to inspire more responsibility through things like welfare reform and child support enforcement. But I have come to believe that unless we can solve the second problem we'll never really solve the first one. Unless we can find a way to honestly and openly debate our differences and find common ground, to celebrate all the diversity of America and still give people a chance to live in the way they think is right, so we are stronger for our differences, not weaker, we won't be able to meet the economic and other challenges before us. And therefore, I have decided that I should spend some more time in some conversations about things Americans care a lot about and that they're deeply divided over.

Today I want to talk about a conversation—about a subject that can provoke a fight in nearly any country town or on any city street corner in America—religion. It's a subject that should not drive us apart. And we have a mechanism as old as our Constitution for bringing us together.

This country, after all, was founded by people of profound faith who mentioned Divine Providence and the guidance of God twice in the Declaration of Independence. They were searching for a place to express their faith freely without persecution. We take it for granted today that that's so in this county, but it was not always so. And it certainly has not always been so across the world. Many of the people who were our first settlers came here primarily because they were looking for a place where they could practice their faith without being persecuted by the government.

Here in Virginia's soil, as secretary of education has said, the oldest and deepest roots of religious liberty can be found. The First Amendment was modeled on Thomas Jefferson's Statutes of Religious Liberty for Virginia. He thought so much of it that he asked that on his gravestone it be said not that he was the president, not that he had been vice president or secretary of state, but that he was the founder of the University of Virginia, the author of the Declaration of Independence, and the author of the Statutes of Religious Liberty for the state of Virginia.

And of course, no one did more than James Madison to

put the entire Bill of Rights in our Constitution, and especially, the First Amendment.

Religious freedom is literally our first freedom. It is the first thing mentioned in the Declaration of Independence. And as it opens, it says Congress cannot make a law that either establishes a religion or restricts the free exercise of religion. Now, as with every provision of our Constitution, that law has had to be interpreted over the years, and it has in various ways that some of us agree with and some of us disagree with. But one thing is indisputable: the First Amendment has protected our freedom to be religious or not religious, as we choose, with the consequence that in this highly secular age the United States is clearly the most conventionally religious country in the entire world, at least the entire industrialized world.

We have more than 250,000 places of worship. More people go to church here every week, or to the synagogue, or to a mosque or other place of worship than in any other country in the world. More people believe religion is directly important to their lives than in any other advanced, industrialized country in the world. And it is not an accident. It is something that has always been a part of our life.

I grew up in Arkansas which is, except for West Virginia, probably the state that's most heavily Southern Baptist Protestant in the country. But we had two synagogues and a Greek Orthodox church in my hometown. Not so long ago in the heart of our agricultural country in eastern Arkansas one of our universities did a big outreach to students in the Middle East, and before you know it, out there on this flat land where there was no building more than two stories high, there rose a great mosque. And all the farmers from miles around drove in to see what the mosque was like and try to figure out what was going on there. (Laughter.)

This is a remarkable country. And I have tried to be faithful to that tradition that we have of the First Amendment. It's something that's very important to me.

Secretary Riley mentioned when I was at Georgetown, Georgetown is a Jesuit school, a Catholic school. All the Catholics were required to teach theology, and those of us who weren't Catholic took a course in world religions, which we called Buddhism for Baptists. (Laughter.) And I began a sort of love affair with the religions that I did not know anything about before that time.

It's a personal thing to me because of my own religious faith and the faith of my family. And I've always felt that in order for me to be free to practice my faith in this country, I had to let other people be as free as possible to practice theirs, and that the government had an extraordinary obligation to bend over backwards not to do anything to impose any set of views on any group of people or to allow others to do it under the cover of the law.

That's why I was very proud—one of the proudest things I've been able to do as president was to sign into law the Religious Freedom Restoration Act in 1993. And it was designed to reverse the decision of the Supreme Court that essentially made it pretty easy for government, in the pursuit of its legitimate objectives, to restrict the exercise of people's religious liberties. This law basically said—I won't use the legalese—the bottom line was that if the government is going to restrict anybody's legitimate exercise of religion they have to have an extraordinarily good reason and no other way to achieve their compelling objective other than to do this. You have to bend over backwards to avoid getting in the way of people's legitimate exercise of their religious convictions. That's what the law said.

This is something I've tried to do throughout my career. When I was governor, for example, we were having—of Arkansas in the '80's, you may remember this—there were religious leaders going to jail in America because they ran child care centers that they refused to have certified by the state because they said it undermined their ministry. We solved that problem in our state. There are people who were prepared to go to jail over the home schooling issue in the '80's because they said it was part of their religious ministry. We solved that problem in our state.

With the Religious Freedom Restoration Act we made it possible, clearly, in areas that were previously ambiguous for Native Americans, for American Jews, for Muslims to practice the full range of their religious practices when they might have otherwise come in contact with some governmental regulation.

And in a case that was quite important to the Evangelicals in our country, I instructed the Justice Department to change our position after the law passed on a tithing case where a family had been tithing to their church and the man declared bankruptcy, and the government took the position they could go get the money away from the church because he knew he was bankrupt at the time he gave it. And I realized in some ways that was a close question, but I thought we had to stand up for the proposition that people should be able to practice their religious convictions.

Secretary Riley and I, in another context, have also learned as we have gone along in this work that all the religions obviously share a certain devotion to a certain set of values which make a big difference in the schools. I want to commend Secretary Riley for his relentless support of the so-called character education movement in our schools, which is clearly led in many schools that had great troubles to reduce drop-out rates, increased performance in schools, better citizenship in ways that didn't promote any particular religious views but at least unapologetically advocated values shared by all major religions.

In this school, one of the reasons I wanted to come here is because I recognize that this work has been done here. There's a course in this school called Combatting Intolerance, which deals not only with racial issues, but also with religious differences, and studies times in the past when people have been killed in mass numbers and persecuted because of their religious convictions.

You can make a compelling argument that the tragic war in Bosnia today is more of a religious war than an ethnic war. The truth is, biologically, there is no difference in the Serbs, the Croats, and the Muslims. They are Catholics, Orthodox Christians, and Muslims, and they are so for historic reasons. But it's really more of a religious war than an ethnic war when properly viewed. And I think it's very important that the people in this school are learning that and, in the progress, will come back to that every great religion teaches honesty and trustworthiness and responsibility and devotion to family, and charity and compassion toward others.

Our sense of our own religion and our respect for others

has really helped us to work together for two centuries. It's made a big difference in the way we live and the way we function and our ability to overcome adversity. The constitution wouldn't be what it is without James Madison's religious values. But it's also, frankly, given us a lot of elbow room. I remember, for example, that Abraham Lincoln was derided by his opponents because he belonged to no organized church. But if you read his writings and you study what happened to him, especially after he came to the White House, he might have had more spiritual depth than any person ever to hold the office that I now have the privilege to occupy.

So we have followed this balance, and it has served us well. Now what I want to talk to you about for a minute is that our Founders understood that religious freedom basically was a coin with two sides. The Constitution protected the free exercise of religion, but prohibited the establishment of religion. It's a careful balance that's uniquely American. It is the genius of the First Amendment. It does not, as some people have implied, make us a religion-free country. It has made us the most religious country in the world.

It does not convert—let's just take the areas of greatest controversy now—all the fights have come over 200 years over what those two things mean: What does it mean for the government to establish a religion, and what does it mean for a government to interfere with the free exercise of religion? The Religious Freedom Restoration Act was designed to clarify the second provision—government interfering with the free exercise of religion and to say you can do that almost never. You can do that almost never. (Applause.)

We have had a lot more fights in the last 30 years over what the government establishment of religion means. And that's what the whole debate is now over the issue of school prayer, religious practices in the schools, and things of that kind. And I want to talk about it because our schools are the places where so much of our hearts are in America and all of our futures are. And I'd like to begin by just sort of pointing out what's going on today and then discussing it if I could. And, again, this is always kind of inflammatory; I want to have a noninflammatory talk about it. (Laughter.)

First of all, let me tell you a little about my personal history. Before the Supreme Court's decision in the Engel against Vitale, which said that the state of New York could not write a prayer that had to be said in every school in New York every day, school prayer was as common as apple pie in my hometown. And when I was in junior high school, it was my responsibility either to start every day by reading the Bible or get somebody else to do it. Needless to say, I exerted a lot of energy in finding someone else to do it from time to time, being a normal 13-year-old-boy.

Now, you could say, well, it certainly didn't do any harm; it might have done a little good. But remember what I told you. We had two synagogues in my hometown. We also had pretended to be deeply religious, and there were no blacks in my school, they were in a segregated school. And I can tell you that all of us who were in there doing it never gave a second thought most of the time to the fact that we didn't have blacks in our schools and that there were Jews in the classroom who were probably deeply offended by half the stuff we were saying or doing—or maybe made to feel inferior.

I say that to make the point that we have not become less

religious over the last 30 years by saying that schools cannot impose a particular religion, even if it's a Christian religion and 98 percent of the kids in the schools are Christian and Protestant. I'm not sure that Catholics were always comfortable with what we did either. We had a big Catholic population in my school and in my hometown. But I did that—I have been a part of this debate we are talking about. This is a part of my personal life experience. So I have seen a lot of progress made and I agreed with the Supreme Court's original decision in Engel v. Vitale.

Now, since then, I've not always agreed with every decision the Supreme Court made in the area of the First Amendment. I said the other day I didn't think the decision on the prayer at the commencement, where the Rabbi was asked to give the nonsectarian prayer at the commencement—I didn't agree with that because I didn't think it any coercion at all. And I thought that people were not interfered with. And I didn't think it amounted to the establishment of a religious practice by the government. So I have always agreed.

But I do believe that on balance, the direction of the First Amendment has been very good for America and has made us the most religious country in the world by keeping the government out of creating religion, supporting particular religions, and interfering with other people's religious practices.

What is giving rise to so much of this debate today I think is two things. One is the feeling that the schools are special and a lot of kids are in trouble, and a lot of kids are in trouble for nonacademic reasons, and we want our kids to have good values and have a good future.

Let me give you just one example. There is today being

released a new study of drug use among young people by the group that Joe Califano was associated with—Council for a Drug-Free America—massive poll of young people themselves. It's a fascinating study and I urge all of you to get it. Joe came in a couple of days ago and briefed me on it. It shows disturbingly that even though serious drug use is down overall in groups in America, casual drug use is coming back up among some of our young people who no longer believe that it's dangerous and have forgotten that it's wrong and are basically living in a world that I think is very destructive.

And I see it all the time. It's coming back up. Even though we're investing money and trying to combat it in education and treatment programs and supporting things like the DARE program. And we're breaking more drug rings than ever before around the world. It's almost—it's very disturbing because it's fundamentally something that is kind of creeping back in.

But the study shows that there are three major causes for young people not using drugs. One is they believe that their future depends upon their not doing it; they're optimistic about the future. The more optimistic kids are about the future, the less likely they are to use drugs.

Second is having a strong, positive relationship with their parents. The closer kids are to their parents and the more tuned in to them they are, and the more their parents are good role models, the less likely kids are to use drugs.

You know what the third is? How religious the children are. The more religious the children are, the less likely they are to use drugs.

So what's the big fight over religion in the schools and what does it mean to us and why are people so upset about it? I think there are basically three reasons. One is, people believe that—most Americans believe that if you're religious, personally religious, you ought to be able to manifest that anywhere at any time, in a public or private place. Second, I think that most Americans are disturbed if they think that our government is becoming antireligious, instead of adhering to the firm spirit of the First Amendment—don't establish, don't interfere with, but respect. And the third thing is people worry about our national character as manifest in the lives of our children. The crime rate is going down in almost every major area in America today, but the threat of violent random crime among very young people is still going up.

So these questions take on a certain urgency today for personal reasons and for larger social reasons. And this old debate that Madison and Jefferson started over 200 years ago is still being spun out today basically as it relates to what can and cannot be done in our schools, and the whole question, specific question, of school prayer, although I would argue it goes way beyond that.

So let me tell you what I think the law is and what we're trying to do about it, since I like the First Amendment, and I think we're better off because of it, and I think that if you have two great pillars—the government can't establish and the government can't interfere with—obviously there are going to be a thousand different factual cases that will arise at any given time, and the courts from time to time will make decisions that we don't all agree with, but the question is, are the pillars the right pillars, and do we more or less come out in the right place over the long run?

The Supreme Court is like everybody else, it's imperfect—

and so are we. Maybe they're right and we're wrong. But we are going to have these differences. The fundamental balance that has been struck it seems to me has been very good for America, but what is not good today is that people assume that there is a positive-antireligious bias in the cumulative impact of these court decisions with which our administration—the Justice Department and the secretary of education and the president—strongly disagree. So let me tell you what I think the law is today and what I have instructed the Department of Education and the Department of Justice to do about it.

The First Amendment does not—I will say again—does not convert our schools into religion-free zones. If a student is told he can't wear a yarmulke, for example, we have an obligation to tell the school the law says the student can, most definitely, wear a yarmulke to school. If a student is told she cannot bring a Bible to school, we have to tell the school, no, the law guarantees her the right to bring a Bible to school.

There are those who do believe our schools should be value-neutral and that religion has no place inside the schools. But I think that wrongly interprets the idea of the wall between church and state. They are not the walls of the school.

There are those who say that values and morals and religions have no place in public education; I think that is wrong. First of all, the consequences of having no values are not neutral. The violence in our streets—not value neutral. The movies we see aren't neutral. Television is not value neutral. Too often we see expressions of human degradation, immorality, violence, and debasement of the human soul that have more influence and take more time and occupy more space in the minds of our young people than any of the influences that are felt at school anyway. Our schools, therefore, must be a barricade against this kind of degradation. And we can do it without violating the First Amendment.

I am deeply troubled that so many Americans feel that their faith is threatened by the mechanisms that are designed to protect their faith. Over the past decade we have seen a real rise in these kinds of cultural tensions in America. Some people even say we have a culture war. There have been books written about culture war, the culture of disbelief, all these sort of trends arguing that many Americans genuinely feel that a lot of our social problems today have arisen in large measure because the country led by the government has made an assault on religious convictions. That is fueling a lot of this debate today over what can and cannot be done in the schools.

Much of the tension stems from the idea that religion is simply not welcome at all in what Professor Carter at Yale has called the public square. Americans feel that instead of celebrating their love for God in public, they're being forced to hide their faith behind closed doors. That's wrong. Americans should never have to hide their faith. But some Americans have been denied the right to express their religion, and that has to stop. That has happened, and it has to stop. It is crucial that government does not dictate or demand specific religious views, but equally crucial that government doesn't prevent the expression of specific religious views.

When the First Amendment is invoked as an obstacle to private expression of religion, it is being misused. Religion has a proper place in private and a proper place in public because the public square belongs to all Americans. It's especially important that parents feel confident that their children can practice religion. That's why some families have been frustrated to see their children denied even the most private forms of religious expression in public schools. It is rare, but these things have actually happened.

I know that most schools do a very good job of protecting students' religious rights, but some students in America have been prohibited from reading the Bible silently in study hall. Some student religious groups haven't been allowed to publicize their meetings in the same way that nonreligious groups can. Some students have been prevented even from saying grace before lunch. That is rare, but it has happened and it is wrong. Wherever and whenever the religious rights of children are threatened or suppressed, we must move quickly to correct it. We want to make it easier and more acceptable for people to express and to celebrate their faith.

Now, just because the First Amendment sometimes gets the balance a little bit wrong in specific decisions by specific people doesn't mean there's anything wrong with the First Amendment. I still believe the First Amendment as it is presently written permits the American people to do what they need to do. That's what I believe. (Applause.) Let me give you some examples and you see if you agree.

First of all, the First Amendment does not require students to leave their religion at the schoolhouse door. We wouldn't want students to leave the values they learn from religion, like honesty and sharing and kindness, behind the schoolhouse door—behind at the schoolhouse door, and reinforcing those values is an important part of every school's mission.

Some school officials and teachers and parents believe that the Constitution forbids any religious expression at all in public schools. That is wrong. Our courts have made it clear that is wrong. It is also not a good idea. Religion is too important to our history and our heritage for us to keep it out of our schools. Once again, it shouldn't be demanded, but as long as it is not sponsored by school officials and doesn't interfere with other children's rights, it mustn't be denied.

For example, students can pray privately and individually whenever they want. They can say grace themselves before lunch. There are times when they can pray out loud together. Student religious clubs in high schools can and should be treated just like any other extracurricular club. They can advertise their meeting, meet on school grounds, use school facilities just as other clubs can. When students can choose to read a book to themselves, they have every right to read the Bible or any other religious text they want.

Teachers can and certainly should teach about religion and the contributions it has made to our history, our values, our knowledge, to our music and our art in our country and around the world, and to the development of the kind of people we are. Students can also pray to themselves—preferably before tests, as I used to do. (Laughter.)

Students should feel free to express their religion and their beliefs in homework, through artwork, during class presentations, as long as it's relevant to the assignment. If students can distribute flyers or pamphlets that have nothing to do with the school, they can distribute religious flyers and pamphlets on the same basis. If students can wear T-shirts advertising sports teams, rock groups, or politicians, they can wear T-shirts that promote religion. If certain subjects or activities are objectionable to their students or their parents because of their religious beliefs, then schools may, and sometimes they must, excuse students from those activities.

Finally, even though the schools can't advocate religious beliefs, as I said earlier, they should teach mainstream values and virtues. The fact that some of these values happen to be religious values does not mean that they cannot be taught in our schools.

All these forms of religious expression and worship are permitted and protected by the First Amendment. That doesn't change the fact that some students haven't been allowed to express their beliefs in these ways. What we have to do is to work together to help all Americans understand exactly what the First Amendment does. It protects freedom of religion by allowing students to pray, and it protects freedom of religion by preventing schools from telling them how and when and what to pray. The First Amendment keeps us all on common ground. We are allowed to believe and worship as we choose without the government telling any of us what we can and cannot do.

It is in that spirit that I am today directing the secretary of education and the attorney general to provide every school district in America before school starts this fall with a detailed explanation of the religious expression permitted in schools, including all things that I've talked about today. I hope parents, students, educators, and religious leaders can use this directive as a starting point. I hope it helps them to understand their differences, to protect students' religious rights, and to find common ground. I believe we can find that common ground.

This past April a broad coalition of religious and legal

groups—Christian and Jewish, conservative and liberal, Supreme Court advocates and Supreme Court critics—put themselves on the solution side of this debate. They produced a remarkable document called "Religion in Public Schools: A Joint Statement of Current Law." They put aside their deep differences and said, we all agree on what kind of religious expression the law permits in our schools. My directive borrows heavily and gratefully from their wise and thoughtful statement. This is a subject that could have easily divided the men and women that came together to discuss it. But they moved beyond their differences, and that may be as important as the specific document they produced.

I also want to mention over 200 religious and civic leaders who signed the Williamsburg Charter in Virginia in 1988. That charter reaffirms the core principles of the First Amendment. We can live together with our deepest differences and all be stronger for it.

The charter signers are impressive in their own right and all the more impressive for their differences of opinion, including Presidents Ford and Carter; Chief Justice Rehnquist and the late Chief Justice Burger; Senator Dole and former Governor Dukakis; Bill Bennett and Lane Kirkland, the president of the AFL-CIO; Norman Lear and Phyllis Schlafly signed it together—(laughter)—Coretta Scott King and Reverend James Dobson.

These people were able to stand up publicly because religion is a personal and private thing for Americans which has to have some public expression. That's how it is for me. I'm pretty old-fashioned about these things. I really do believe in the constancy of sin and the constant possibility of forgiveness, the reality of redemption and the promise of a future life. But I'm also a Baptist who believes that salvation is primarily personal and private, that my relationship is directly with God and not through any intermediary.

People—other people can have different views. And I've spent a good part of my life trying to understand different religious views, celebrate them and figure out what brings us together.

I will say again, the First Amendment is a gift to us. And the Founding Fathers wrote the Constitution in broad ways so that it could grow and change, but hold fast to certain principles. They knew—they knew that all people were fallible and would make mistakes from time to time. And I have—as I said, there are times when the Supreme Court makes a decision, if I disagree with it, one of us is wrong. There's another possibility: both of us could be wrong. (Laughter.) That's the way it is in human affairs.

But what I want to say to the American people and what I want to say to you is that James Madison and Thomas Jefferson did not intend to drive a stake in the heart of religion and to drive it out of our public life. What they intended to do was to set up a system so that we could bring religion into our public life and into our private life without any of us telling the other what to do.

This is a big deal today. One county in America, Los Angeles County, has over 150 different racial and ethnic groups in it—over 150 different. How many religious views do you suppose are in those groups? How many? Every significant religion in the world is represented in significant numbers in one American county, and many smaller religious groups—in one American county.

We have got to get this right. We have got to get this right. And we have to keep this balance. This country needs to be a place where religion grows and flourishes.

Don't you believe that if every kid in every difficult neighborhood in America were in a religious institution on the weekends, the synagogue on Saturday, a church on Sunday, a mosque on Friday, don't you really believe that the drug rate, the crime rate, the violence rate, the sense of self-destruction would go way down and the quality of the character of this country would go way up? (Applause.)

But don't you also believe that if for the last 200 years we had a state-governed religion, people would be bored with it, think that it would—(laughter and applause)—they would think it had been compromised by politicians, shaved around the edges, imposed on people who didn't really consent to it, and we wouldn't have 250,000 houses of worship in America? (Applause.) I mean, we wouldn't.

It may be perfect—imperfect, the First Amendment, but it is the nearest thing ever created in any human society for the promotion of religious values because it left us free to do it. And I strongly believe that the government has made a lot of mistakes which we have tried to roll back in interfering with that around the edges. That's what the Religious Freedom Restoration Act is all about. That's what this directive that Secretary Riley and the Justice Department and I have worked so hard on is all about. That's what our efforts to bring in people of different religious views are all about. And I strongly believe that we have erred when we have rolled it back too much. And I hope that we can have a partnership with our churches in many ways to reach out to the young people who need the values, the hope, the belief, the convictions that come with faith, and the sense of security in a very uncertain and rapidly changing world.

But keep in mind we have a chance to do it because of the heritage of America and the protection of the First Amendment. We have to get it right.

Thank you very much. (Applause.)

Memorandum from President Bill Clinton on Religious Expression in Public Schools

For the Secretary of Education and the Attorney General

Religious freedom is perhaps the most precious of all American liberties—called by many our "first freedom." Many of the first European settlers in North America sought refuge from religious persecution in their native countries. Since that time, people of faith and religious institutions have played a central role in the history of this Nation. In the First Amendment, our Bill of Rights recognizes the twin pillars of religious liberty: the constitutional protection for the free exercise of religion, and the constitutional prohibition on the establishment of religion by the state. Our Nation's founders knew that religion helps to give our people the character without which a democracy cannot survive. Our founders also recognized the need for a space of freedom between government and the people—that the government must not be permitted to coerce the conscience of an individual or group.

In over 200 years since the First Amendment was included in our Constitution, religion and religious institutions have thrived throughout the United States. In 1993, I was proud to reaffirm the historic place of religion. I signed the Religious Freedom Restoration Act, which restores a high legal standard to protect the exercise of religion from being inappropriately burdened by government action. In the greatest traditions of American citizenship, a broad coalition of individuals and organizations came together to support the fullest protection for religious practice and expression.

Religious Expression in Public Schools

I share the concern and frustration that many Americans feel about situations where the protections accorded by the First Amendment are not recognized or understood. This problem has manifested itself in our Nation's public schools. It appears that some school officials, teachers, and parents have assumed that religious expression of any type is either inappropriate, or forbidden altogether, in public schools.

As our courts have reaffirmed, however, nothing in the First Amendment converts our public schools into religion-free zones, or requires all religious expression to be left behind at the schoolhouse door. While the government may not use schools to coerce the consciences of our students, or to convey official endorsement of religion, the government's schools also may not discriminate against private religious expression during the school day.

I have been advised by the Department of Justice and the

Department of Education that the First Amendment permits—and protects—a greater degree of religious expression in public schools than many Americans may now understand. The Departments of Justice and Education have advised me that, while application may depend upon specific factual contexts and will require careful consideration in particular cases, the following principles are among those that apply to religious expression in our schools:

Students' prayer and religious discussion: The Establishment Clauses of the First Amendment does not prohibit purely private religious speech by students. Students therefore have the same right to engage in individual or group prayer and religious discussion during the school day as they do to engage in other comparable activity. For example, students may read their Bibles or other scriptures, say grace before meals, and pray before tests to the same extent they may engage in comparable non-disruptive activities. Local school authorities possess substantial discretion to impose rules of order and other pedagogical restrictions on student activities, but they may not structure or administer such rules to discriminate against religious activity or speech.

Generally, students may pray in a nondisruptive manner when not engaged in school activities or instruction, and subject to the rules that normally pertain in the application setting. Specifically, students in informal settings, such as cafeterias and hallways, may pray and discuss their religious views with each other, subject to the same rules or order as apply to other student activities and speech. Students may also speak to, and attempt to persuade, their peers about religious topics just as they do with regard to political topics. School officials, however, should intercede to stop students' speech that constitutes harassment aimed at a student or a group of students.

Students may also participate in before or after school events with religious content, such as "see you at the flag pole" gatherings, on the same terms as they may participate in other noncurriculum activities on school premises. School officials may neither discourage nor encourage participation in such an event.

The right to engage in voluntary prayer or religious discussion free form discrimination does not include the right to have a captive audience listen, or to compel other students to participate. Teachers and school administrators should ensure that no student is in any way coerced to participate in religious activity.

Graduation prayer and baccalaureates: Under current Supreme Court decisions, school officials may not mandate or organize prayer at graduation, nor organize religious baccalaureate ceremonies. If a school generally opens its facilities to private groups, it must make its facilities available on the same terms to organizers of privately sponsored religious baccalaureate services. A school may not extend preferential treatment to baccalaureate ceremonies and may in some instances be obligated to disclaim official endorsement of such ceremonies.

Official neutrality regarding religious activity: Teachers and school administrators, when acting in those capacities, are representatives of the state and are prohibited by the establishment clause from soliciting or encouraging religious activity and from participating in such activity with students. Teachers and administrators also are prohibited from discouraging activity because of its religious content, and from soliciting or encouraging antireligious activity.

Teaching about religion: Public schools may not provide religious instruction, but they may teach *about* religion, including the Bible or other scripture: the history of religion, comparative religion, the Bible (or other scripture) as literature, and the role of religion in the history of the United States and other countries all are permissible public school subjects. Similarly, it is permissible to consider religious influences on art, music, literature, and social studies. Although public schools may teach about religious holidays, including their religious aspects, and may celebrate the secular aspects of holidays, schools may not observe holidays as religious events or promote such observance by students.

Student assignments: Students may express their beliefs about religion in the form of homework, artwork, and other written and oral assignments free of discrimination based on the religious content of their submissions. Such home and classroom work should be judged by ordinary academic standards of substance and relevance, and against other legitimate pedagogical concerns identified by the school.

Religious literature: Students have a right to distribute religious literature to their schoolmates on the same terms as they are permitted to distribute other literature that is unrelated to the school curriculum or activities. Schools may impose the same reasonable time, place, and manner or other constitutional restrictions on distribution of religious literature as they do on nonschool literature generally, but they may not single out religious literature for special regulation.

Religious excusals: Subject to applicable State laws, schools enjoy substantial discretion to excuse individual students from lessons that are objectionable to the student or the students' parents on religious or other conscientious grounds. School officials may neither encourage nor discourage students from availing themselves of an excusal option. Under the Religious Freedom Restoration Act, if it is proved that particular lessons substantially burden a student's free exercise of religion and if the school cannot prove a compelling interest in requiring attendance, the school would be legally required to excuse the student.

Released time: Subject to applicable State laws, schools have the discretion to dismiss students to off-premises religious instruction, provided that schools do not encourage or discourage participation or penalize those who do not attend. Schools may not allow religious instruction by outsiders on school premises during the school day.

Teaching values: Though schools must be neutral with respect to religion, they may play an active role with respect to teaching civic values and virtue, and the moral code that holds us together as a community. The fact that some of these values are held also by religions does not make it unlawful to teach them in school.

Student garb: Students may display religious messages on items of clothing to the same extent that they are permitted to display other comparable messages. Religious messages may not be singled out for suppression, but rather are subject to the same rules as generally apply to comparable messages. When wearing particular attire, such as yarmulkes and head scarves, during the school day is part of students' religious practice, under the Religious Freedom Restoration Act schools generally may not prohibit the wearing of such items.

I hereby direct the Secretary of Education, in consultation with the Attorney General, to use appropriate means to ensure that public school districts and school officials in the United States are informed, by the start of the coming school year, of the principles set forth above.

The Equal Access Act

The Equal Access Act is designed to ensure that, consistent with the First Amendment, student religious activities are accorded the same access to public school facilities as are student secular activities. Based on decisions of the Federal courts, as well as its interpretations of the Act, the Department of Justice has advised me of its position that the Act should be interpreted as providing, among other things, that:

General provisions: Student religious groups at public secondary schools have the same right of access to school facilities as is enjoyed by other comparable student groups. Under the Equal Access Act, a school receiving Federal funds that allows one or more student noncurriculum-related clubs to meet on its premises during noninstructional time may not refuse access to student religious groups.

Prayer services and worship exercises covered: A meeting, as defined and protected by the Equal Access Act, may include a prayer service, Bible reading, or other worship exercises.

Equal access to means of publicizing meetings: A school receiving Federal funds must allow student groups meeting under the Act to use the school media—including the public address system, the school newspaper, and the school bulletin board—to announce their meetings on the same terms as other noncurriculum-related student groups are allowed to use the school media. Any policy concerning the use of school media must be applied to all noncurriculum-related student groups in a nondiscriminatory matter. Schools, however, may inform students that certain groups are not school sponsored.

Lunch-time and recess covered: A school creates a limited open forum under the Equal Access Act, triggering equal access rights for religious groups, when it allows students to meet during their lunch periods or other noninstructional time during the school day, as well as when it allows students to meet before and after the school day.

I hereby direct the Secretary of Education, in consultation with the Attorney General, to use appropriate means to ensure that public school districts and school officials in the United States are informed, by the start of the coming school year, of these interpretations of the Equal Access Act.

William J. Clinton

Letter from Jay Sekulow on Violations of the Equal Access Act

February 15, 1994

The Honorable Janet Reno
Attorney General of the United States
10th and Constitution Avenues NW
Washington, D.C. 20530

The Honorable Richard W. Riley
Secretary of Education
United States Department of Education
400 Maryland Avenue SW
Washington, D.C. 20202

re: Patterns of Violations of the Equal Access Act, Title 20 U.S.C. 4071 *et seq.*

Dear General Reno and Secretary Riley:

On behalf of the American Center for Law and Justice, I am writing this letter to bring to your attention a problem of continuing violations of federal civil rights in the educational setting. I hope that the Departments of the federal government under your supervision will examine with care the problem about which I write, and take appropriate steps to remedy the abuses that compel this correspondence. By way of introduction, the undersigned attorney served as counsel of record before the Supreme Court of the United States in two matters directly related to the subject of this letter, arguing for the student Respondents in Board of Education of Westside Community Schools v. Bridget Mergens, 496 U.S. 226 (1990) and arguing for the Church Petitioner in Lamb's Chapel v. Center Moriches Union Free School District, 113 S. Ct. 2141 (1993).

As you recall, in 1984, the Ninety-Eighth Congress passed, and the President signed legislation entitled "the Equal Access Act," P.L. 98-377, 98 Stat. 1303, 20 U.S.C. 4071 *et seq.* The Act "was intended to address perceived widespread discrimination against religious speech in public schools. . . ." *Board of Education of Westside Community Schools v. Bridget Mergens,* 496 U.S. 226 (1990). The Equal Access Act makes it unlawful for

> any public secondary school which receives Federal financial assistance and which has a limited open forum to deny equal access or a fair opportunity to, or discriminate against, any students who wish to conduct a meeting within that limited open forum on the basis of the religious, political, philosophical, or other content of the speech at such meetings. [20 U.S.C. 4071 (a)]

Congress specifically considered the constitutionality of the Act under the Establishment Clause prior to enactment, and the Supreme Court confirmed the constitutionality of the Act in the above-cited decision in *Board of Education of Westside Community Schools v. Bridget Mergens.* The United States Department of Justice intervened in the *Mergens* case before the United States Supreme Court, arguing for the constitutionality of the Act. Consequently, the Act has been reviewed by all three branches of the federal government for possible constitutional difficulty, and its constitutionality has clearly been established.

Given the uncontroverted status of the Equal Access Act, it would seem that local public school compliance with the requirements of the Act would be a foregone conclusion. Regrettably, such has not been the case. Staff attorneys with the American Center for Law and Justice are confronted daily by situations in which local school districts flagrantly disobey the Act and thereby, violate the civil rights of public secondary school students who have sought access to their schools' club forum in order to form a Bible club or prayer group. The Center provides free legal assistance to public secondary students whose rights under the act to initiate Bible clubs or prayer groups have been denied. For your information, and to help demonstrate the continuing breadth of the problem, I have attached to this letter a chart which summarizes some eighty-five incidents that occurred in the last four months in which the Center has provided assistance to public school students. See "Recent Incidents Evidencing Violations of the Federal Equal Access Act," attached as Exhibit A hereto.

As you can see from the "Recent Incidents" exhibit, students from around the Nation are continuing to suffer deprivations of rights protected by federal law. Exhibit A documents more than 80 incidents in the last four months alone in which students rights have been violated by school districts in derogation of the Act. The harms inflicted vary from school to school—many school districts have completely denied the right to form a Bible club, others have denied students equality in access to the public address system, the yearbook and other means of advertising.

To assist students whose federal civil rights have been violated, our attorneys correspond with, and make presentations to, school boards around the Nation. Often, our efforts to educate public secondary school officials leads to appropriate resolutions. Not every incident, however, resolves amicably. Indeed, just this week, the Center will file federal civil rights litigation in Virginia and in New York to seek redress on behalf of students in two school districts which have persisted, after being apprised of the Act and its requirements, in denying equal access for student-initiated, student-led Bible clubs. For your information I have attached to this letter copies of the Complaints from filed in both lawsuits. See "Verified Complaint in *Jackie Marie Ferguson v. Isle of Wight County School Board,*" attached hereto as Exhibit B; "Verified Complaint in *Emily Hsu v. Roslyn Union Free School District No. 3,*" attached hereto as Exhibit C.

As these attachments demonstrate, the demand for equality expressed in the enactment of the Equal Access Act has not become everyday reality for students in all public schools which are recipients of federal funding. This problem disturbs us, and, we trust that it troubles you as well. I have concluded that your departments, of Justice and of Education, are the proper ones to investigate the problem of continuing violations of the Equal Access Act and to take corrective action, including appropriate rule-making. At a minimum, it seems fitting that the Civil Rights Division of the Justice Department investigate these matters and that the Education Department adopt regulations requiring school district recipients of federal funding to certify their compliance with the requirements of the Act.

Our organization stands ready to assist your inquiries into this matter. I look forward to the favor of a reply.

Very truly yours,
The American Center for Law and Justice
by: Jay Sekulow
Jay Alan Sekulow
Chief Counsel

News Release on Violations of the Equal Access Act

Immediate Release
February 16, 1994
Contact: Gene Kapp
(804) 523-7111

Attorney General, Requested to Protect Students' Civil Rights

(Washington, D.C.)—U.S. Attorney General Janet Reno and Secretary of Education Richard Riley have been asked to intervene in school districts across the country which are violating the federal civil rights of students who are being denied access to participate in constitutionally protected religious activities at school.

The request came today—in a national news conference—

from the American Center for Law and Justice, a Virginia-based public interest law firm and educational organization which has initiated an aggressive legal campaign by filing lawsuits against offending school districts nationwide.

"School districts across America have developed a cavalier attitude toward the First Amendment rights of students on campus," said Jay Sekulow, Chief Counsel of the ACLJ. "There's an open hostility to constitutionally-protected religious activities in the schools, and we're asking the Justice and Education Departments to step-in and provide assistance to stop it."

At issue: a growing number of public school districts that refuse to permit students to participate in prayer groups or Bible clubs. In this school year alone, Sekulow says the ACLJ has received requests for assistance in 82 school districts in 28 states, and has now gone to court in Virginia and New York over the issue.

Sekulow said: "The number of violations which are cropping up around the country is alarming. It's time for the federal government to step-in and protect the free speech rights of all students—including those with religious beliefs."

The ACLJ contends the federal civil rights of students are being violated in several ways:

1) SCHOOL DISTRICTS ARE IGNORING THE EQUAL ACCESS ACT. The Act makes it unlawful for any public school that receives federal funding, and allows non-curriculum clubs to meet on campus to deny equal access to any students who wish to conduct a meeting

"on the basis of the religious, political, philosophical, to other content of the speech" at the meetings.

2) SCHOOL DISTRICTS ARE DENYING STUDENTS' FIRST AMENDMENT RIGHTS. In 1990, the U.S. Supreme Court upheld the constitutionality of the Equal Access Act in the case of *Westside Community Schools v. Mergens,* which allowed Bible clubs or prayer groups to meet on public school campuses.

"The growing wave of intolerance against people of faith must be stopped," said Keith Fournier, Executive Director of the ACLJ. "It's a threat to everyone—even those who do not believe. It strikes at the heart of the nature of liberty in a constitutional democracy."

In a letter delivered today to Attorney General Reno and Education Secretary Riley, Sekulow—who successfully argued the *Mergens* case before the Supreme Court—urged the Civil Rights Division of the Justice Department to conduct an investigation, and appealed to the Education Department to make school districts who receive federal funds prove that they are complying with the Equal Access Act.

The ACLJ filed suit today in U.S. District Court in Norfolk, Va. and in U.S. District Court for Eastern District of New York on behalf of high school students who have been denied permission to take part in Bible clubs in their schools.

In Virginia, the ACLJ is suing the Isle of Wight County School Board because two students from Smithfield High School were denied permission to form a Bible club. In New York, the case involves two students who were denied permission to start a Bible club at Roslyn High School in Roslyn

Heights, New York. In both cases, the ACLJ is asking for injunctive relief to bring an end to the illegal actions of the school districts.

ACLJ Chief Counsel Sekulow says more lawsuits are likely: "There's a new belligerent attitude that defies the imagination. We will not hesitate to send legal SWAT teams anywhere in the country to protect the free speech rights of students."

ACLJ's Fournier says the request to get the federal government involved is an important move in protecting students' rights too: "One of the proper roles of government is to defend the constitutionally-protected rights of its citizenry. That's why we're asking the federal government to intervene on behalf of all students who, because of their religious beliefs, are being denied equal access."

Both Sekulow and Fournier say they believe there are several reasons why there's a growing hostility toward religion in schools: first, students are becoming more aware of their First Amendment rights and exercising them and secondly, there's an organized campaign of misinformation and disinformation to give both students and school administrators the wrong impression concerning the legality of student-led and student-initiated prayer in public school.

In addition to supplying the Justice and Education Departments with information about the violations of the Equal Access Act, the ACLJ will send information to the White House and each member of Congress.

The American Center for Law and Justice is a public interest law firm and educational organization based in Virginia Beach, Va. The ACLJ has a national network of affiliate attorneys with offices in Washington, D.C., Atlanta, Phoenix, as well as New Hope, Kentucky and Mobile, Alabama.

For further information, contact: Gene Kapp at (804) 523-7111.

Letter from a Birmingham Jail

An Introduction by Jay Alan Sekulow and Keith A. Fournier

Dr. Martin Luther King, Jr.'s "Letter from a Birmingham Jail" is now recognized both as a masterpiece of Christian literature and as an eloquent statement of the meaning of Christian civil disobedience. In light of the current struggle for Christian rights in the school system, marketplace, and at sites of social protest, his letter takes on renewed relevance.

Dr. King's thoughts are an important guide for current Christian activism and litigation. We recognize Martin Luther King, Jr., as one of the greatest Christian leaders of this century. His writings impart profound insight and encouragement in the current pro-life struggle. Such significance led the American Center for Law and Justice to offer the letter on the nationally broadcasted "Jay Sekulow Live!" radio program.

The document was prefaced with comments by the Reverend Paul Chaim Schenck, executive vice president and chief of operations of the American Center for Law and Justice (ACLJ). Most significantly, the Reverend Schenck's introduction was written while he was in jail for civil disobedience. During incarceration for participation in Operation Rescue's protest of abortion clinics in Buffalo, Reverend Schenck found Dr. King's comments to be particularly comforting and meaningful. Ultimately, King and his family paid a high price for his bold stand.

Schenck is an apt symbol of the thousands of pro-lifers who have been battered by the courts for their participation in the nonviolent struggle to save the unborn.

Standing for the Truth

Dressed in clerical collars, Robert and Paul Schenck are very difficult to distinguish from each other. Rob is slighter and has different glasses from his ten-minutes-younger brother. The twins are ministers of the gospel, both equally committed to a nonviolent stand against abortion. They have dedicated their lives to the cause, been arrested together, stood next to each other in jail.

Paul made the headlines of the *Buffalo News* on Sunday, April 19, 1992, after going to an area near an abortion clinic to prepare spiritually for the next day's Spring of Life protest. As he knelt in prayer, two hundred pro-choice advocates stood in front of the GYN Womenservices clinic. They charged forward, pushing and shoving Paul. His glasses flew from his head, and his Bible was knocked from his hands. As they pummelled the minister, he fell backward. Cigarettes were put out in his hair. The crowd began spitting.

Insults and jeering continued unabated as the women spit.

Soon Paul's face, neck, and shirt were completely sopped. He said nothing but continued praying.

The police stood by and did nothing.

Sara Lolar, spokesperson for National Women's Rights Organizing Coalition (NWROC), said, "We aren't into looking respectable and not swearing. We don't just let them sit there and pray." The NWROC was a two-year-old group describing itself as militant and left wing, dedicated to keeping abortion legal.[1]

Lolar set the parameters for discussion by declaring that the use of violence might be the most effective way to keep abortion in effect. "Society is willing to fight [for abortion rights]. Violence is a necessary fact. Sometimes it is needed."[2]

In contrast, Reverend Paul Schenck did nothing but keep responding, "God bless you. God bless you."

The Showdown in Buffalo

The photo of angry women screaming in the serene face of Paul Schenck filled the cover of the July 1992 *Life* magazine.

Explaining the motivation behind the march on the abortion clinic, Reverend Joe Slovence, a regional director of Operation Rescue, said, "When we lay down our bodies before the killing chambers, our bodies become living sacrifices to God. You may experience a little discomfort in jail but no one's going to rip your head off or pull your arms and legs off, which is what they do to the children."[3]

As a matter of record, 617 pro-lifers were arrested during the Spring of Life protests in Buffalo. Reverend Paul Schenck's legal problems continued for years after the event. But the results were more than worth the effort. Over 6,000 supporters joined in, many first-timers. Twenty women contemplating abortion changed their minds.

Elaine Mroz was moved by what she saw in the television report and came down to join the protests. An emergency room nurse in Clarence, New York, Mroz said, "The courage they showed made me come out to the clinics. Back in my college days I wondered how people allowed the Holocaust to happen. I see the same pattern here. And I don't want anyone asking me someday, 'What did you do about abortion?'"[4]

Sixteen-year-old Stephanie White, four months pregnant with twins, was going to the Erie Medical Center for an abortion, but someone in the crowd handed her a pamphlet. She remembers thinking, "Why should I go through with this abortion when there are people who are going to help me?"[5]

On What Authority?

What caused the Schenck brothers' passionate involvement in the cause? In Paul's introduction to the special edition of the Birmingham Jail Letter, he described the highly significant place Scripture had in his life. In addition, his parents raised his brother and sisters to be sensitive to the blacks' civil rights struggle during the days of Martin Luther King's own protests. Paul, who was called Chaim—in Hebrew, the word for *life*, grew up thinking of Dr. King not as a dangerous radical or agitator but as a minister of the gospel doing what God called him to do. However, a particular event shaped Chaim's unyielding commitment to civil disobedience as a necessary response to the abortion crisis.

A plastic bag filled with medical wastes was fished out of the trash and placed on Reverend Schenck's desk. Inside he found the end results of abortion: the remaining pieces of unborn life, the butchered remnants of the promise of a future generation. The experience shook him to the core. Chaim remembers, "I found myself thrusting my hands into the mess trying to reassemble body parts." He could no longer be an observer of the social massacre created by *Roe v. Wade.*

Reasons for Defiance

But reasoned Christian response must be based on more than the feelings of moral outrage. When Jesus promised that the meek would inherit the earth, He was speaking of the need for restraint and carefully focused behavior arising from sound theological basis. In fact, Robert and Paul Schenck acted out of a significant philosophical and theological perspective, shaped by the meaning of the cross of Jesus Christ.

Dr. King's letter offers lessons to help galvanize outrage into constructive action. As you read the letter, the following observations will help you identify how King turned Christian theology into a focused force for social change still providing direction for pro-lifers and other Christians involved in protests.

Keith has said many times, "There is no question that abortion is the great moral injustice of the age. Human beings are reduced to nothing more than things." You can observe that Dr. King's letter refers to the writing of the Jewish philosopher Martin Buber. Buber wrote that human beings must be seen as "thous" and never reduced to inanimate "its." When King spoke of the depersonalization of segregation, he could have been identically describing what happens as an unborn child is reduced to an "it." The sacred creation of God becomes only a mass of tissue.

(If you were the fetus about to be terminated without opportunity to plead for your life, would you consider yourself the victim of the worst possible injustice?)

The Highest Respect for the Highest Law

Civil disobedience is rooted in a profound respect for eternal law and the conviction that all human beings are created in the image of God. King noted that any law that uplifts human personality is just; any law that degrades life is unjust. Ultimate allegiance to the laws of God is the motivating force behind all civil disobedience. Christians recognize that human laws must square first and foremost with the law of God or they cannot be obeyed.

The ACLJ exists to bring unjust laws into the light of God's truth. We stand with and behind all persons who will not be compromised by anything less than the total truth.

It is no mistake of history that the civil rights movement was centered in the church. Dr. King was the product of the gospel tradition that teaches that every human being is of supreme worth. The same value given to black citizens must be given to every form of human life. Civil disobedience reflects the conviction that all law exists to serve life and not the opposite.

True Injustice

Jay observes, "Today pro-lifers are being treated differently in the courts than are other people. Such abuse is true biblical injustice." Not only does judicial prejudice offend the law of God, it is contrary to the best tradition of this country's legal system. Yale law professor Steven Carter has pointed out that the current popular image of the pro-life movement is an example of cultural and legal confusion. He notes that a movement with a spiritual base cannot be considered inappropriate because it pursues a spiritual end. Pro-life protestors stand in a long line of Christian witnesses that have fought for truth in all of the important struggles of Western civilization.

Nonviolence

Christian protest seeks to speak and act out the truth in the context of love. Dr. King's letter makes the ultimate point. Every form of violence must be shunned. Christian civil disobedience harms no one.

Keith notes, "Our willingness to sacrifice ourselves in the struggle is the essence of the Christian faith." Keith often speaks of both white and red martyrdom. "When we die for the cause we are swept up with the glorious company of the martyrs of blood. But white sacrifice is the daily business of being willing to be behind bars if necessary, to be misunderstood and maligned in the cause without ever reacting with violence." King's letter helps us understand why this stance is often our only possible alternative.

The Reverend Johnny Hunter, recipient of the Southern Christian Leadership Conference's Dr. Martin Luther King nonviolence award, believes the most significant aspect of the King legacy is the manner in which rhetoric was turned into activity. He said, "In the spirit of Dr. King, there comes a time when we decide who we will obey. We must obey Christ and help our brothers and sisters. We may have to go to jail when the judicial system crosses a line that is wrong." Reverend

Hunter reminds us that all such crossings are done nonviolently.

Extremists?

But are pro-life protestors unbalanced radicals only looking for a rationale for their actions?

Martin Luther King's letter describes Jesus Christ as the original extremist. Calvary was an example of extremism in the quest to express the radical love of God. Obviously, the first Christians were also considered dangerously immoderate.

We must remember that the charge of extremism is relative. Labelers usually call those who disagree with them extreme rather than consider the ideas the protestors are presenting. Consider the actions of some German citizens during the Third Reich. Would we not view those protesting the extermination of Jews to be politically radical? The Nazis not only did, they placed such persons in the same death camps with Jews. Future generations may look back on our society's current failure to protest the death of the unborn as a similar lack of moral vision and courage.

Founder of Operation Rescue, Randall Terry said on "Jay Sekulow Live!": "Our adversaries in this cultural war want to bludgeon us into silence. They want to intimate us until we say their ideas have merit. The Sixth Commandment forbids murder. When we say abortion is murder and must be stopped, they call us 'extremist.'"

Parallels

Paul Chaim Schenck has called our attention to the current parallels between the pro-life movement and the civil rights struggle. As you read King's letter, substitute "pro-life movement" for "civil rights movement." The closed lunch counters of the 1960s are today's abortion clinics and hospitals that routinely snuff out life in the womb. As blacks were segregated earlier in the century, today the unborn are being segregated out of life. Segregation is the a priori form of what *Roe v. Wade* did in robbing the preborn of personhood. Terms such as *tissue* and *pregnancy products,* like the derogatory labels that racists give blacks, are selected to reduce human beings to nothing more than "its."

However, as in King's letter written over thirty years ago, sadly, "Christian" is still "Christian" and the "church" is still the "church." Dr. King didn't fear the Klan or the white supremacists but church people who believed segregation was immoral and did nothing. The current sleeping church still faces the same challenge of the Gospel of Christ, the Gospel of advocacy and action.

Letter from a Birmingham Jail

April 16, 1963

MY DEAR FELLOW CLERGYMEN:

While confined here in the Birmingham city jail, I came across your recent statement calling my present activities "unwise and untimely." Seldom do I pause to answer criticism of my work and ideas. If I sought to answer all the criticisms that cross my desk, my secretaries would have little time for anything other than such correspondence in the course of the day, and I would have no time for constructive work. But since I feel that you are men of genuine good will and that your criticisms are sincerely set forth, I want to try to answer your statements in what I hope will be patient and reasonable terms.

I think I should indicate why I am here in Birmingham, since you have been influenced by the view which argues against "outsiders coming in." I have the honor of serving as president of the Southern Christian Leadership Conference, an organization operating in every southern state, with headquarters in Atlanta, Georgia. We have some eighty-five affiliated organizations across the South, and one of them is the Alabama Christian Movement for Human Rights. Frequently we share staff, educational and financial resources with our affiliates. Several months ago the affiliate here in Birmingham asked us to be on call to engage in a nonviolent direct-action program if such were deemed necessary. We readily consented, and when the hour came we lived up to our promise. So I, along with several members of my staff, am here because I was invited here. I am here because I have organizational ties here.

But more basically, I am in Birmingham because injustice is here. Just as the prophets of the eighth century B.C. left their villages and carried their "thus saith the Lord" far beyond the boundaries of their home towns, and just as the Apostle Paul left his village of Tarsus and carried the gospel of Jesus Christ to the far corners of the Greco-Roman world, so am I compelled to carry the gospel of freedom beyond my own home town. Like Paul, I must constantly respond to the Macedonian call for aid.

Moreover, I am cognizant of the interrelatedness of all communities and states. I cannot sit idly by in Atlanta and not be concerned about what happens in Birmingham. Injustice anywhere is a threat to justice everywhere. We are caught in an inescapable network of mutuality, tied in a single garment of destiny. Whatever affects one directly, affects all indirectly. Never again can we afford to live with the narrow, provincial "outside agitator" idea. Anyone who lives inside the United States can never be considered an outsider anywhere within its bounds.

You deplore the demonstrations taking place in Birmingham. But your statement, I am sorry to say, fails to express a similar concern for the conditions that brought about the demonstrations. I am sure that none of you would want to rest content with the superficial kind of social analysis that deals merely with effects and does not grapple with underlying causes. It is unfortunate that demonstrations are taking place in Birmingham, but it is even more unfortunate that the city's white power structure left the Negro community with no alternative.

In any nonviolent campaign there are four basic steps: collection of the facts to determine whether injustices exist; negotiation; self-purification; and direct action. We have gone through all these steps in Birmingham. There can be no gainsaying the fact that racial injustice engulfs this community. Birmingham is probably the most thoroughly segregated city in the United States. Its ugly record of brutality is widely known. Negroes have experienced grossly unjust treatment in the courts. There have been more unsolved bombings of Negro homes and churches in Birmingham than in any other city in the nation. These are the hard, brutal facts of the case. On the basis of these conditions, Negro leaders sought to negotiate with the city fathers.

But the latter consistently refused to engage in good-faith negotiation.

Then, last September, came the opportunity to talk with leaders of Birmingham's economic community. In the course of the negotiations, certain promises were made by the merchants—for example, to remove the stores' humiliating racial signs. On the basis of these promises, the Reverend Fred Shuttlesworth and the leaders of the Alabama Christian Movement for Human Rights agreed to a moratorium on all demonstrations. As the weeks and months went by, we realized that we were the victims of a broken promise. A few signs, briefly removed, returned; the others remained.

As in so many past experiences, our hopes bad been blasted, and the shadow of deep disappointment settled upon us. We had no alternative except to prepare for direct action, whereby we would present our very bodies as a means of laying our case before the conscience of the local and the national community. Mindful of the difficulties involved, we decided to undertake a process of self-purification. We began a series of workshops on nonviolence, and we repeatedly asked ourselves, "Are you able to accept blows without retaliation?" "Are you able to endure the ordeal of jail?" We decided to schedule our direct-action program for the Easter season, realizing that except for Christmas, this is the main shopping period of the year. Knowing that a strong economic-withdrawal program would be the by-product of direct action, we felt that this would be the best time to bring pressure to bear on the merchants for the needed change.

Then it occurred to us that Birmingham's mayoralty election was coming up in March, and we speedily decided to postpone action until after election day. When we discovered that the Commissioner of Public Safety, Eugene "Bull" Connor, had piled up enough votes to be in the run-off we decided again to postpone action until the day after the run-off so that the demonstrations could not be used to cloud the issues. Like many others, we waited to see Mr. Connor defeated, and to this end we endured postponement after postponement. Having aided in this community need, we felt that our direct-action program could be delayed no longer.

You may well ask: "Why direct action? Why sit-ins, marches and so forth? Isn't negotiation a better path?" You are quite right in calling, for negotiation. Indeed, this is the very purpose of direct action. Nonviolent direct action seeks to create such a crisis and foster such a tension that a community which has constantly refused to negotiate is forced to confront the issue. It seeks so to dramatize the issue that it can no longer be ignored. My citing the creation of tension as part of the work of the nonviolent-resister may sound rather shocking. But I must confess that I am not afraid of the word "tension." I have earnestly opposed violent tension, but there is a type of constructive, nonviolent tension which is necessary for growth. Just as Socrates felt that it was necessary to create a tension in the mind so that individuals could rise from the bondage of myths and half-truths to the unfettered realm of creative analysis and objective appraisal, we must we see the need for nonviolent gadflies to create the kind of tension in society that will help men rise from the dark depths of prejudice and racism to the majestic heights of understanding and brotherhood.

The purpose of our direct-action program is to create a

situation so crisis-packed that it will inevitably open the door to negotiation. I therefore concur with you in your call for negotiation. Too long has our beloved Southland been bogged down in a tragic effort to live in monologue rather than dialogue.

One of the basic points in your statement is that the action that I and my associates have taken in Birmingham is untimely. Some have asked: "Why didn't you give the new city administration time to act?" The only answer that I can give to this query is that the new Birmingham administration must be prodded about as much as the outgoing one, before it will act. We are sadly mistaken if we feel that the election of Albert Boutwell as mayor will bring the millennium to Birmingham. While Mr. Boutwell is a much more gentle person than Mr. Connor, they are both segregationists, dedicated to maintenance of the status quo. I have hope that Mr. Boutwell will be reasonable enough to see the futility of massive resistance to desegregation. But he will not see this without pressure from devotees of civil rights. My friends, I must say to you that we have not made a single gain in civil rights without determined legal and nonviolent pressure. Lamentably, it is an historical fact that privileged groups seldom give up their privileges voluntarily. Individuals may see the moral light and voluntarily give up their unjust posture; but, as Reinhold Niebuhr has reminded us, groups tend to be more immoral than individuals.

We know through painful experience that freedom is never voluntarily given by the oppressor; it must be demanded by the oppressed. Frankly, I have yet to engage in a direct-action campaign that was "well timed" in the view of those who have not suffered unduly from the disease of segregation. For years now I have heard the word "Wait!" It rings in the ear of every Negro with piercing familiarity. This "Wait" has almost always meant "Never." We must come to see, with one of our distinguished jurists, that "justice too long delayed is justice denied."

We have waited for more than 340 years for our constitutional and God-given rights. The nations of Asia and Africa are moving with jetlike speed toward gaining political independence, but we still creep at horse-and-buggy pace toward gaining a cup of coffee at a lunch counter. Perhaps it is easy for those who have never felt the stinging dark of segregation to say, "Wait." But when you have seen vicious mobs lynch your mothers and fathers at will and drown your sisters and brothers at whim; when you have seen hate-filled policemen curse, kick and even kill your black brothers and sisters; when you see the vast majority of your twenty million Negro brothers smothering in an airtight cage of poverty in the midst of an affluent society; when you suddenly find your tongue twisted and your speech stammering as you seek to explain to your six-year-old daughter why she can't go to the public amusement park that has just been advertised on television, and see tears wailing up in her eyes when she is told that Funtown is closed to colored children, and see ominous clouds of inferiority beginning to form in her little mental sky, and see her beginning to distort her personality by developing an unconscious bitterness toward white people; when you have to concoct an answer for a five-year-old son who is asking: "Daddy, why do white people treat colored people so mean?"; when you take a cross-county drive and find it necessary to sleep night after night in the uncomfortable corners of your automobile because no motel will accept you; when you are humiliated day in and day out by nagging signs reading "white" and "colored"; when your first name becomes "nigger," your middle name becomes "boy" (however old you are) and your last name becomes "John," and your wife and mother are never given the respected title "Mrs."; when you are harried by day and haunted by night by the fact that you are a Negro, living constantly at tiptoe stance, never quite knowing what to expect next, and are plagued with inner fears and outer resentments; when you are forever fighting a degenerating sense of "nobodiness" then you will understand why we find it difficult to wait. There comes a time when the cup of endurance runs over, and men are no longer willing to be plunged into the abyss of despair. I hope, sirs, you can understand our legitimate and unavoidable impatience.

You express a great deal of anxiety over our willingness to break laws. This is certainly a legitimate concern. Since we so diligently urge people to obey the Supreme Court's decision of 1954 outlawing segregation in the public schools, at first glance it may seem rather paradoxical for us consciously to break laws. One may well ask: "How can you advocate breaking some laws and obeying others?" The answer lies in the fact that there are two types of laws: just and unjust. I would be the Brat to advocate obeying just laws. One has not only a legal but a moral responsibility to obey just laws. Conversely, one has a moral responsibility to disobey unjust laws. I would agree with St. Augustine that "an unjust law is no law at all."

Now, what is the difference between the two? How does one determine whether a law is just or unjust? A just law is a man-made code that squares with the moral law or the law of

God. An unjust law is a code that is out of harmony with the moral law. To put it in the terms of St. Thomas Aquinas: An unjust law is a human law that is not rooted in eternal law and natural law. Any law that uplifts human personality is just. Any law that degrades human personality is unjust. All segregation statutes are unjust because segregation distorts the soul and damages the personality. It gives the segregator a false sense of superiority and the segregated a false sense of inferiority. Segregation, to use the terminology of the Jewish philosopher Martin Buber, substitutes an "I-it" relationship for an "I-thou" relationship and ends up relegating persons to the status of things. Hence segregation is not only politically, economically and sociologically unsound, it is morally wrong and awful. Paul Tillich said that sin is separation. Is not segregation an existential expression of man's tragic separation, his awful estrangement, his terrible sinfulness? Thus it is that I can urge men to obey the 1954 decision of the Supreme Court, for it is morally right; and I can urge them to disobey segregation ordinances, for they are morally wrong.

Let us consider a more concrete example of just and unjust laws. An unjust law is a code that a numerical or power majority group compels a minority group to obey but does not make binding on itself. This is difference made legal. By the same token, a just law is a code that a majority compels a minority to follow and that it is willing to follow itself. This is sameness made legal.

Let me give another explanation. A law is unjust if it is inflicted on a minority that, as a result of being denied the right to vote, had no part in enacting or devising the law. Who can say that the legislature of Alabama which set up that state's segregation laws was democratically elected? Throughout Alabama all sorts of devious methods are used to prevent Negroes from becoming registered voters, and there are some counties in which, even though Negroes constitute a majority of the population, not a single Negro is registered. Can any law enacted under such circumstances be considered democratically structured?

Sometimes a law is just on its face and unjust in its application. For instance, I have been arrested on a charge of parading without a permit. Now, there is nothing wrong in having an ordinance which requires a permit for a parade. But such an ordinance becomes unjust when it is used to maintain segregation and to deny citizens the First Amendment privilege of peaceful assembly and protest.

I hope you are able to see the distinction I am trying to point out. In no sense do I advocate evading or defying the law, as would the rabid segregationist. That would lead to anarchy. One who breaks an unjust law must do so openly, lovingly, and with a willingness to accept the penalty. I submit that an individual who breaks a law that conscience tells him is unjust and who willingly accepts the penalty of imprisonment in order to arouse the conscience of the community over its injustice, is in reality expressing the highest respect for law.

Of course, there is nothing new about this kind of civil disobedience. It was evidenced sublimely in the refusal of Shadrach, Meshach and Abednego to obey the laws of Nebuchadnezzar, on the ground that a higher moral law was at stake. It was practiced superbly by the early Christians, who were willing to face hungry lions and the excruciating pain of chopping blocks rather than submit to certain unjust laws of the Roman Empire. To a degree, academic freedom is a reality today because Socrates practiced civil disobedience. In our own nation, the Boston Tea Party represented a massive act of civil disobedience.

We should never forget that everything Adolf Hitler did in Germany was "legal" and everything the Hungarian freedom fighters did in Hungary was "illegal." It was "illegal" to aid and comfort a Jew in Hitler's Germany. Even so, I am sure that, had I lived in Germany at the time, I would have aided and comforted my Jewish brothers. If today I lived in a Communist country where certain principles dear to the Christian faith are suppressed, I would openly advocate disobeying that country's antireligious laws.

I must make two honest confessions to you, my Christian and Jewish brothers. First, I must confess that over the past few years I have been gravely disappointed with the white moderate. I have almost reached the regrettable conclusion that the Negro's great stumbling block in his stride toward freedom is not the White Citizen's Councilor or the Ku Klux Klanner, but the white moderate, who is more devoted to "order" than to justice; who prefers a negative peace which is the absence of tension to a positive peace which is the presence of justice; who constantly says: "I agree with you in the goal you seek, but I cannot agree with your methods of direct action"; who paternalistically believes he can set the timetable for another man's freedom; who lives by a mythical concept of time and who constantly advises the Negro to wait for a "more convenient season." Shallow understanding from people of good will is more frustrating than absolute misunderstanding from people of ill will. Lukewarm acceptance is much more bewildering than outright rejection.

I had hoped that the white moderate would understand that law and order exist for the purpose of establishing justice and that when they fan in this purpose they become the dangerously structured dams that block the flow of social progress. I had hoped that the white moderate would understand that the present tension in the South is a necessary phase of the transition from an obnoxious negative peace, in which the Negro passively accepted his unjust plight, to a substantive and positive peace, in which all men will respect the dignity and worth of human personality. Actually, we who engage in nonviolent direct action are not the creators of tension. We merely bring to the surface the hidden tension that is already alive. We bring it out in the open, where it can be seen and dealt with. Like a boil that can never be cured so long as it is covered up but must be opened with all its ugliness to the natural medicines of air and light, injustice must be exposed, with all the tension its exposure creates, to the light of human conscience and the air of national opinion before it can be cured.

In your statement you assert that our actions, even though peaceful, must be condemned because they precipitate violence. But is this a logical assertion? Isn't this like condemning a robbed man because his possession of money precipitated the evil act of robbery? Isn't this like condemning Socrates because his unswerving commitment to truth and his philosophical inquiries precipitated the act by the misguided populace in which they made him drink hemlock? Isn't this like condemning Jesus because his unique God-consciousness and never-ceasing devotion to God's will precipitated the evil act of crucifixion? We must come to see that, as the federal courts have consistently affirmed, it is wrong to urge an individual to cease his efforts to gain his basic constitutional rights because the quest may precipitate violence. Society must protect the robbed and punish the robber.

I had also hoped that the white moderate would reject the myth concerning time in relation to the struggle for freedom. I have just received a letter from a white brother in Texas. He writes: "All Christians know that the colored people will receive equal rights eventually, but it is possible that you are in too great a religious hurry. It has taken Christianity almost two thousand years to accomplish what it has. The teachings of Christ take time to come to earth." Such an attitude stems from a tragic misconception of time, from the strangely rational notion that there is something in the very flow of time that will inevitably cure all ills. Actually, time itself is neutral; it can be used either destructively or constructively. More and more I feel that the people of ill will have used time much more effectively than have the people of good will. We will have to repent in this generation not merely for the hateful words and actions of the bad people but for the appalling silence of the good people. Human progress never rolls in on wheels of inevitability; it comes through the tireless efforts of men willing to be co-workers with God, and without this hard work, time itself becomes an ally of the forces of social stagnation. We must use time creatively, in the knowledge that the time is always ripe to do right. Now is the time to make real the promise of democracy and transform our pending national elegy into a creative psalm of brotherhood. Now is the time to lift our national policy from the quicksand of racial injustice to the solid rock of human dignity.

You speak of our activity in Birmingham as extreme. At fist I was rather disappointed that fellow clergymen would see my nonviolent efforts as those of an extremist. I began thinking about the fact that I stand in the middle of two opposing forces in the Negro community. One is a force of complacency, made up in part of Negroes who, as a result of long years of oppression, are so drained of self-respect and a sense of "somebodiness" that they have adjusted to segregation; and in part of a few middle class Negroes who, because of a degree of academic and economic security and because in some ways they profit by segregation, have become insensitive to the problems of the masses. The other force is one of bitterness and hatred, and it comes perilously close to advocating violence. It is expressed in the various black nationalist groups that are springing up across the nation, the largest and best-known being Elijah Muhammad's Muslim movement. Nourished by the Negro's frustration over the continued existence of racial discrimination, this movement is made up of people who have lost faith in America, who have absolutely repudiated Christianity, and who have concluded that the white man is an incorrigible "devil."

I have tried to stand between these two forces, saying that we need emulate neither the "do-nothingism" of the complacent nor the hatred and despair of the black nationalist. For there is the more excellent way of love and nonviolent protest. I am grateful to God that, through the influence of the Negro church, the way of nonviolence became an integral part of our struggle.

If this philosophy had not emerged, by now many streets of the South would, I am convinced, be flowing with blood. And I am further convinced that if our white brothers dismiss as "rabble-rousers" and "outside agitators" those of us who employ nonviolent direct action, and if they refuse to support our nonviolent efforts, millions of Negroes will, out of frustration and despair, seek solace and security in black-nationalist ideologies, a development that would inevitably lead to a frightening racial nightmare.

Oppressed people cannot remain oppressed forever. The yearning for freedom eventually manifests itself, and that is what has happened to the American Negro. Something within has reminded him of his birthright of freedom, and something without has reminded him that it can be gained. Consciously or unconsciously, he has been caught up by the Zeitgeist, and with his black brothers of Africa and his brown and yellow brothers of Asia, South America and the Caribbean, the United States Negro is moving with a sense of great urgency toward the promised land of racial justice. If one recognizes this vital urge that has engulfed the Negro community, one should readily understand why public demonstrations are taking place. The Negro has many pent-up resentments and latent frustrations, and he must release them. So let him march; let him make prayer pilgrimages to the city hall; let him go on freedom rides-and try to understand why he must do so. If his repressed emotions are not released in nonviolent ways, they will seek expression through violence; this is not a threat but a fact of history. So I have not said to my people: "Get rid of your discontent." Rather, I have tried to say that this normal and healthy discontent can be channeled into the creative outlet of nonviolent direct action. And now this approach is being termed extremist.

But though I was initially disappointed at being categorized as an extremist, as I continued to think about the matter I gradually gained a measure of satisfaction from the label. Was not Jesus an extremist for love: "Love your enemies, bless them that curse you, do good to them that hate you, and pray for them which despitefully use you, and persecute you." Was not Amos an extremist for justice: "Let justice roll down like waters and righteousness like an ever-flowing stream." Was not Paul an extremist for the Christian gospel: "I bear in my body the marks of the Lord Jesus." Was not Martin Luther an extremist: "Here I stand; I cannot do otherwise, so help me God." And John Bunyan: "I will stay in jail to the end of my days before I make a butchery of my conscience." And Abraham Lincoln: "This nation cannot survive half slave and half free." And Thomas Jefferson: "We hold these truths to be self-evident, that an men are created equal . . . " So the question is not whether we will be extremists, but what kind of extremists we will be. Will we be extremists for hate or for love? Will we be extremists for the preservation of injustice or for the extension of justice? In that dramatic scene on Calvary's hill three men were crucified. We must never forget that all three were crucified for the same crime—the crime of extremism. Two were extremists for immorality, and thus fell below their environment. The other, Jesus Christ, was an extremist for love, truth and goodness, and thereby rose above his environment. Perhaps the South, the nation and the world are in dire need of creative extremists.

I had hoped that the white moderate would see this need.

Perhaps I was too optimistic; perhaps I expected too much. I suppose I should have realized that few members of the oppressor race can understand the deep groans and passionate yearnings of the oppressed race, and still fewer have the vision to see that injustice must be rooted out by strong, persistent and determined action. I am thankful, however, that some of our white brothers in the South have grasped the meaning of this social revolution and committed themselves to it. They are still too few in quantity, but they are big in quality. Some—such as Ralph McGill, Lillian Smith, Harry Golden, James McBride Dabbs, Ann Braden and Sarah Patton Boyle—have written about our struggle in eloquent and prophetic terms. Others have marched with us down nameless streets of the South. They have languished in filthy, roach-infested jails, suffering the abuse and brutality of policemen who view them as "dirty nigger lovers." Unlike so many of their moderate brothers and sisters, they have recognized the urgency of the moment and sensed the need for powerful "action" antidotes to combat the disease of segregation.

Let me take note of my other major disappointment. I have been so greatly disappointed with the white church and its leadership. Of course, there are some notable exceptions. I am not unmindful of the fact that each of you has taken some significant stands on this issue. I commend you, Reverend Stallings, for your Christian stand on this past Sunday, in welcoming Negroes to your worship service on a nonsegregated basis. I commend the Catholic leaders of this state for integrating Spring Hill College several years ago.

But despite these notable exceptions, I must honestly reiterate that I have been disappointed with the church. I do not say this as one of those negative critics who can always find something wrong with the church. I say this as a minister of the gospel, who loves the church; who was nurtured in its bosom; who has been sustained by its spiritual blessings and who will remain true to it as long as the cord of Rio shall lengthen.

When I was suddenly catapulted into the leadership of the bus protest in Montgomery, Alabama, a few years ago, I felt we would be supported by the white church, felt that the white ministers, priests and rabbis of the South would be among our strongest allies. Instead, some have been outright opponents, refusing to understand the freedom movement and misrepresenting its leaders; and too many others have been more cautious than courageous and have remained silent behind the anesthetizing security of stained-glass windows.

In spite of my shattered dreams, I came to Birmingham with the hope that the white religious leadership of this community would see the justice of our cause and, with deep moral concern, would serve as the channel through which our just grievances could reach the power structure. I had hoped that each of you would understand. But again I have been disappointed.

I have heard numerous southern religious leaders admonish their worshipers to comply with a desegregation decision because it is the law, but I have longed to hear white ministers declare: "Follow this decree because integration is morally right and because the Negro is your brother." In the midst of blatant injustices inflicted upon the Negro, I have watched white churchmen stand on the sideline and mouth pious irrelevancies and sanctimonious trivialities. In the midst of a mighty struggle to rid our nation of racial and economic injustice, I have heard many ministers say: "Those are social issues, with which the gospel has no real concern." And I have watched many churches commit themselves to a completely other worldly religion which makes a strange, un-Biblical distinction between body and soul, between the sacred and the secular.

I have traveled the length and breadth of Alabama, Mississippi and all the other southern states. On sweltering summer days and crisp autumn mornings I have looked at the South's beautiful churches with their lofty spires pointing heavenward. I have beheld the impressive outlines of her massive religious-education buildings. Over and over I have found myself asking: "What kind of people worship here? Who is their God? Where were their voices when the lips of Governor Barnett dripped with words of interposition and nullification? Where were they when Governor Walleye gave a clarion call for defiance and hatred? Where were their voices of support when bruised and weary Negro men and women decided to rise from the dark dungeons of complacency to the bright hills of creative protest?"

Yes, these questions are still in my mind. In deep disappointment I have wept over the laxity of the church. But be assured that my tears have been tears of love. There can be no deep disappointment where there is not deep love. Yes, I love the church. How could I do otherwise? l am in the rather unique position of being the son, the grandson and the great-grandson of preachers. Yes, I see the church as the body of Christ. But, oh! How we have blemished and scarred that body through social neglect and through fear of being nonconformists.

There was a time when the church was very powerful in the time when the early Christians rejoiced at being deemed worthy to suffer for what they believed. In those days the church was not merely a thermometer that recorded the ideas and principles of popular opinion; it was a thermostat that transformed the mores of society. Whenever the early Christians entered a town, the people in power became disturbed and immediately sought to convict the Christians for being "disturbers of the peace" and "outside agitators." But the Christians pressed on, in the conviction that they were "a colony of heaven," called to obey God rather than man. Small in number, they were big in commitment. They were too God intoxicated to be "astronomically intimidated." By their effort and example they brought an end to such ancient evils as infanticide and gladiatorial contests.

Things are different now. So often the contemporary church is a weak, ineffectual voice with an uncertain sound. So often it is an archdefender of the status quo. Far from being disturbed by the presence of the church, the power structure of the average community is consoled by the church's silent and often even vocal sanction of things as they are.

But the judgment of God is upon the church as never before. If today's church does not recapture the sacrificial spirit of the early church, it will lose its authenticity, forfeit the loyalty of millions, and be dismissed as an irrelevant social club with no meaning for the twentieth century. Every day I meet young people whose disappointment with the church has turned into outright disgust.

Perhaps I have once again been too optimistic. Is organized religion too inextricably bound to the status quo to save our nation and the world? Perhaps I must turn my faith to the inner spiritual church, the church within the church, as the true ekklesia and the hope of the world. But again I am thankful to God that some noble souls from the ranks of organized religion have broken loose from the paralyzing chains of conformity and joined us as active partners in the struggle for freedom. They have left their secure congregations and walked the streets of Albany, Georgia, with us. They have gone down the highways of the South on tortuous rides for freedom. Yes, they have gone to jail with us. Some have been dismissed from their churches, have lost the support of their bishops and fellow ministers. But they have acted in the faith that right defeated is stronger than evil triumphant. Their witness has been the spiritual salt that has preserved the true meaning of the gospel in these troubled times. They have carved a tunnel of hope through the dark mountain of disappointment.

I hope the church as a whole will meet the challenge of this decisive hour. But even if the church does not come to the aid of justice, I have no despair about the future. I have no fear about the outcome of our struggle in Birmingham, even if our motives are at present misunderstood. We will reach the goal of freedom in Birmingham, and all over the nation, because the goal of America is freedom. Abused and scorned though we may be, our destiny is tied up with America's destiny. Before the pilgrims landed at Plymouth, we were here. Before the pen of Jefferson etched the majestic words of the Declaration of Independence across the pages of history, we were here. For more than two centuries our forebears labored in this country without wages; they made cotton king; they built the homes of their masters while suffering gross injustice and shameful humiliation—and yet out of a bottomless vitality they continued to thrive and develop. If the inexpressible cruelties of slavery could not stop us, the opposition we now face will surely fail. We will win our freedom because the sacred heritage of our nation and the eternal will of God are embodied in our echoing demands.

Before closing I feel impelled to mention one other point in your statement that has troubled me profoundly. You warmly commended the Birmingham police force for keeping "order" and "preventing violence." I doubt that you would have so warmly commended the police force if you had seen its dogs sinking their teeth into unarmed, nonviolent Negroes. I doubt that you would so quickly commend the policemen if you were to observe their ugly and inhumane treatment of Negroes here in the city jail; if you were to watch them push and curse old Negro women and young Negro girls; if you were to see them slap and kick old Negro men and young boys; if you were to observe them, as they did on two occasions, refuse to give us food because we wanted to sing our grace together. I cannot join you in your praise of the Birmingham police department.

It is true that the police have exercised a degree of discipline in handling the demonstrators. In this sense they have conducted themselves rather "nonviolently" in pubic. But for what purpose? To preserve the evil system of segregation. Over the past few years I have consistently preached that nonviolence demands that the means we use must be as pure as the ends we seek. I have tried to make clear that it is wrong to use immoral means to attain moral ends. But now I must affirm that it is just as wrong, or perhaps even more so, to use moral means to preserve immoral ends. Perhaps Mr. Connor and his policemen have been rather nonviolent in public, as was Chief Pritchett in Albany, Georgia, but they have used the moral means of nonviolence to maintain the immoral end of racial injustice. As T. S. Eliot has said: "The last temptation is the greatest treason: To do the right deed for the wrong reason."

I wish you had commended the Negro sit-inners and demonstrators of Birmingham for their sublime courage, their willingness to suffer and their amazing discipline in the midst of great provocation. One day the South will recognize its real heroes. They will be the James Merediths, with the noble sense of purpose that enables them to face jeering, and hostile mobs, and with the agonizing loneliness that characterizes the life of the pioneer. They will be old, oppressed, battered Negro women, symbolized in a seventy-two-year-old woman in Montgomery, Alabama, who rose up with a sense of dignity and with her people decided not to ride segregated buses, and who responded with ungrammatical profundity to one who inquired about her weariness: "My feets is tired, but my soul is at rest." They will be the young high school and college students, the young ministers of the gospel and a host of their elders, courageously and nonviolently sitting in at lunch counters and willingly going to jail for conscience' sake. One day the South will know that when these disinherited children of God sat down at lunch counters, they were in reality standing up for what is best in the American dream and for the most sacred values in our Judaeo-Christian heritage, thereby bringing our nation back to those great wells of democracy which were dug deep by the founding fathers in their formulation of the Constitution and the Declaration of Independence.

Never before have I written so long a letter. I'm afraid it is much too long to take your precious time. I can assure you that it would have been much shorter if I had been writing from a comfortable desk, but what else can one do when he is alone in a narrow jail cell, other than write long letters, think long thoughts and pray long prayers?

If I have said anything in this letter that overstates the truth and indicates an unreasonable impatience, I beg you to forgive me. If I have said anything that understates the truth and indicates my having a patience that allows me to settle for anything less than brotherhood, I beg God to forgive me.

I hope this letter finds you strong in the faith. I also hope that circumstances will soon make it possible for me to meet each of you, not as an integrationist or a civil rights leader but as a fellow clergyman and a Christian brother. Let us all hope that the dark clouds of racial prejudice will soon pass away and the deep fog of misunderstanding will be lifted from our fear-drenched communities, and in some not too distant tomorrow the radiant stars of love and brotherhood will shine over our great nation with all their scintillating beauty.

Yours for the cause of Peace and Brotherhood,

Martin Luther King, Jr.

Notes

Chapter 2

1. Habakkuk 2:3.

Chapter 3

1. Bryce J. Christensen, *Utopia Against the Family: The Problems and Politics of the American Family* (San Francisco: Ignatius Press, 1990), 12.
2. Ibid., 22.
3. 343 U.S. 306.
4. William J. Federer, *America's God and Country Encyclopedia of Quotations* (Coppell, Tex.: Fame Publishing, 1994), 9697.
5. J. Moss Ives, *The Ark and the Dove* (New York: Cooper Square Publishers, 1969), 119.
6. Ibid.
7. William T. Davis, ed., *History of the Plymouth Plantation* (New York: Charles Scribner's Sons, 1908), 46.
8. *The Code of 1650*, Being A Compilation of the Earliest Laws and Orders of the General Court of Connecticut (Hartford: Silus Andrus, 1822), 92-93.
9. Acts 22:1; 25:16; 1 Corinthians 9:3; 2 Corinthians 7:11; Philippians 1:7, 16; 2 Timothy 4:16; 1 Peter 3:15.
10. *Liturgy of the Hours* (New York: Catholic Books, 1976), 3:1447.

11. Cardinal James Hickey, "Population Stabilization: Cardinals' Letter Blasts Clinton," American Political Network, Abortion Report, 1 June 1994.

Chapter 4

1. *West Virginia v. Barnette,* 319 U.S. 624 (1943).
2. Catherine Kanner, "America's Anti-Faith Bigots," *Los Angeles Times,* November 7, 1993.
3. "People of Faith in America Shouldn't Be Catching All This Hell," *Houston Chronicle,* October 3, 1993.
4. Ibid.

Chapter 5

1. *Lamb's Chapel and John Steigerwald, Petitioners v. Center Moriches Union Free School District, et al.;* transcript at 35, at 5, 6.
2. Ibid., 47 at 1-10.
3. For more information on this case see Paul Chaim Schenck and Robert L. Schenck, *The Extermination of Christianity: A Tyranny of Consensus* (Lafayette, La.: Huntington House, 1993), 145-50.
4. Oral Arguments Transcript at 62.
5. *Westside Community Schools v. Mergens,* 496 U.S. 226, 250 (1990) (emphasis in original).
6. *Widmar v. Vincent,* 454 U.S. 263 (1981).
7. William J. Bennett, *The Index of Leading Cultural Indicators* (New York: Simon & Schuster, 1994).

8. William J. Bennett, "Getting Used to Decadence: The Spirit of Democracy in Modern America," a lecture delivered on December 7, 1993, at a special meeting of the Heritage Foundation's President's Club, the Heritage Lectures series, number 477, p. 3.

9. Pat Robertson, *The Turning of the Tide: The Fall of Liberalism and the Rise of Common Sense* (Dallas: Word, 1993), 21, 192, 214; Keith A. Fournier, *A House United? Evangelicals and Catholics Together* (Colorado Springs: Liberty, Life & Family/Nav Press, 1994), 121. See also Bennett, "Getting Used to Decadence."

Chapter 6

1. Jack Kelly, "Survey: God Didn't Die—Even Under Socialism," *USA TODAY,* May 18, 1993, 9A.

2. *Westside Community Schools v. Mergens,* 496 U.S. 248 (1990).

3. *Tinker v. Des Moines Independent Community School District,* 393 U.S. 506 (1969).

4. Tinker at 506.

5. *McDaniel v. Paty,* 435 U.S. 618, 641 (1978).

Chapter 7

1. John J. Dunphy, *Humanist,* 1983 (or *Intimidation to Victory,* 83).

2. 370 U.S. 421 (1962) at 425.

3. 374 U.S. at 223.

4. 374 U.S. at 22.

5. 393 U.S. 503 (1969) at 506.

6. Idem. at 504.

7. Jay Sekulow, *Knowing Your Rights* (Colorado Springs: Liberty, Life & Family/Nav Press, 1993), 24.

Chapter 8

1. Barbara J. Syska, Thomas W. Hilgers, and Dennis O'Hare, "An Objective Model for Estimating Criminal Abortions and Its Implications for Public Policy," in *New Perspectives on Human Abortion,* eds. Thomas Hilgers, Dennis J. Horan, and David Mall (Frederick, Md.: University Publications of America, 1981), 178.

2. U.S. Department of Health and Human Services, Centers for Disease Control, Abortion Surveillance Report, May 1983; Merrill McLoughlin, "America's New Civil War," *U.S. News and World Report,* October 3, 1988, 24.

3. Thomas A. Glessner, *Achieving an Abortion-Free America by 2001* (Portland, Oreg.: Multnomah, 1990), 23.

4. Samuel Maull, "Doctor Convicted of Maiming Child in Abortion Try," *Beacon Journal,* February 25, 1993, A4.

5. Kerry Dougherty, "The Time is NOW for Linda William," *Virginian-Pilot/Ledger Star,* January 17, 1993, 11.

6. John Courtney Murray, *We Hold These Truths* (Kansas City, Mo.: Sheed & Ward, 1960), 12.

7. Ibid.

8. Stephen Kinzer, "German Court Restricts Abortion Angering Feminists and the East," *New York Times,* May 29, 1993, 1, 3.

9. Keith A. Fournier, "The Machinery of Death and Justice Blackmun," American Center for Law and Justice, (P.O. Box 64429, 1000 Regent University Drive, Virginia Beach, Va.), February 22, 1994.

10. Thomas Patrick Monaghan, "The Abiding Unconstitutionality and Illegitimacy of *Roe v. Wade," Liberty, Life and Family, An Interdisciplinary Journal of Common Concerns* (P.O. Box 64429, 1000 Regent University Drive, Virginia Beach, Va.) 1994, 1:121.

11. Ibid., 127-28.

Chapter 9

1. Bennett, "Getting Used to Decadence."

2. Ibid.

3. Dorothy Sayers, *The Whimsical Christian* (New York: Macmillan, 1978), 175-76.

4. William Bennett, "Quantifying America's Decline," *Wall Street Journal,* March 15, 1993, A22.

5. Keith A. Fournier, "The 'P.C. Police' Are Watching You," *Law and Justice: The Journal of the American Center for Law and Justice,* vol. 1, no. 4 (Summer 1992): 1.

6. Glenn Ellen Duncan, "The Brain-Snatchers," *Catholic World Report* (March 1993): 54-57.

7. Ibid., 55.

8. Ibid.
9. Tim Friend and Marilyn Elias, "Fetus's Eggs May Become Fertility Aid," *USA Today,* January 4, 1994, 1.
10. Milton Heifetz, *The Right to Die* (New York: Putnam, 1975), 51.
11. Peter Singer, *Practical Ethics* (Cambridge: Cambridge University Press, 1979), 123.
12. Joseph Fletcher, "Infanticide and the Ethics of Loving Concern," in *Infanticide and the Value of Life,* ed. Marvin Kohl (1978), 17, as quoted in *Fighting for Life: Defending the Newborn's Right to Live* (Ann Arbor, Mich.: Servant Books, 1984), 11.
13. B. D. Cohen, as quoted by Nat Hentoff in the *Village Voice,* December 19, 1983.
14. Associated Press Report, *Ann Arbor News,* April 17, 1983.
15. Manney and Blattner, *Death in the Nursery,* 22-23.
16. J. Kerby Anderson, "A Biblical Appraisal of Euthanasia," in *Living Ethically in the 90's,* ed. J. Kerby Anderson (Wheaton, Ill.: Victor Books, 1990), 193-99.
17. "Hospice Offers 'Dignified Death,'" *Paper* (April 1993): 5.
18. George M. Burnell, M.D., *Final Choices: To Live or to Die in an Age of Medical Technology* (New York: Plenium Press, 1933), 33.

19. Jack Kevorkian, as quoted in "Medicide: The Goodness of Planned Death," in *Free Inquiry* (Fall 1991): 14, 17.

20. Sarah Sullivan, "Kevorkian: The Rube Goldberg of Planned Death," in *Cornerstone,* vol. 19. no. 93 (September 1990): 6.

Chapter 10

1. Free Speech Advocates, A Project of Catholics United for Life (New Hope, Ky.), June 1993, 1.
2. *Linda Paquette v. Regal Art Press, Inc.,* Franklin Superior Court, Docket NO. S173-91Fc.
3. Romans 13:1-7.
4. Kokinda, 497 U.S. 720, 733-34 (1990).
5. *Scheider v. State,* 308 U.S. 147 (1939).
6. *Hague v. Committee for Industrial Organization,* 307 U.S. 496, 515 (1939).
7. Idem. at 516.

Chapter 11

1. Acts 17:13-34.
2. Acts 25:10-11.

Chapter 12

1. ADF Briefing, August 1995, Vol. 1, No. 3.
2. "ACLU v. Charity," *Law and Justice: A Publication of the American Center for Law and Justice,* vol. 4, no. 5, p. 1.

3. "Evangelicals and Catholics Together: The Christian Mission in the Third Millennium," as reprinted in Keith A. Fournier with William D. Watkins, *A House United? Evangelicals and Catholics Together—A Winning Alliance for the 21st Century* (Colorado Springs, Colo.: Nav Press; Virginia Beach, Va.: Liberty, Life and Family, 1994), "Appendix," paragraph 30.
4. Ibid., paragraph 20.

Appendix E

1. Jane Kwiatkowski, "Rev. Schenck Shoved Outside Abortion Clinic," *Buffalo News,* April 19, 1992, 1.
2. Ibid.
3. Jeannie Ralston, "The Great Divide," *Life,* July 1992, 36.
4. Ibid., 34.
5. Ibid., 42.

Index